SHAKESPEARE

1700–1740

SHAKESPEARE

1700–1740

A COLLATION OF THE
EDITIONS AND SEPARATE PLAYS
with some account of
T. JOHNSON and R. WALKER

By H. L. FORD

BENJAMIN BLOM   New York / London

T O

The Memory of

R. Crompton Rhodes

Oct. 3, 1935

Alas! for the crystal goblet shattered,
I mingle my tears with yours.

First Published 1935
Reissued 1968
by Benjamin Blom, Inc. Bronx, New York 10452
and 56 Doughty Street London, W.C. 1

Library of Congress Catalog Card Number 68-56498

Printed in the United States of America

CONTENTS

ADDENDA AND CORRIGENDA

Page 25. An unusual state of volume 1 of Pope's second edition in 10 volumes has just· come to hand in the original binding. The 10 vol. title is followed by that of the 8 vol. edition (p. 23); this is evidently a slip on the publisher's part in not removing it when substituting the other title.

Page 37, *line* 23 *should read* ' it is this volume that Rowe '.

Page 120. *The title of* 232 Caius Marius *should read exactly as* 231 a.

Nos. 9, 266, and 303 were also issued in a set of Dryden's works only just unearthed with the following imprint to volume 1 : ' London : | Printed for J. Tonson : And Sold by R. Knaplock, | W. Taylor, W. Mears, J. Browne, W. Churchill, | E. Symon, and J. Brotherton. MDCCXVII.' (*S.*)

It contains Congreve's dedication and so antedates that in the 1718, but *All for Love* is unaltered ; *The Tempest* and *Troilus and Cressida* appear to be identical in each of the three sets of 1717, 1718.

There has been no fitting opportunity to collate 'The Tragical History of King Richard the Third' included in the PLAYS WRITTEN BY MR. CIBBER. In Two Volumes. London ; Printed for Jacob Tonson, over against Catherine-Street in the Strand; Bernard Lintott, at the Cross-Keys between the Temple-Gates in Fleetstreet; William Mears, at the Lamb, without Temple-Bar; and William Chetwood, at Cato's-Head, Russel-Street Covent-Garden. M.DCC.XXI. 2 *vols., 4to.*

Considering the comparative scarcity of the Poems published by B. Lintott, *c.* 1709, it is remarkable that the volume figures in the advertisement on the verso of the half-title to R. Owen's *Hypermnestra*, Lintot, 1722; it is priced at 2*s.* 6*d.* (*S.*)

SUPPLEMENTARY ADDENDA
AND CORRIGENDA

Page 56.   A few notes may prove of interest on 12 volumes of the plays published by Scheurleer in 1750 just lately come to hand. They comprise Nos. II, IV, V, VI, VII, X to XVI, all are dated 1750, and the only variant in these volume-titles is that 'Plais' is so printed in Nos. II, V, and X. The 4 plays in each volume are consecutively irregular in respect to other similarly numbered volumes, as previously stated. Many of the plays are the original dated remainders of those printed in 1710, 1712, 1714, 1718, 1721, 1730, and 1731, and there is one only just then published. About half of them are the undated 'Printed for the Company', and these, if accompanied with one of his devices, may be assigned to the 1720–30 period; but should this imprint be all in capitals and with no device or at most a common example, the date may be safely deemed to be 1731 or later. About 1730 Johnson used a fresh ornament to his titles, namely, a sun framed in a decoration after the Chinese style then in vogue, and such is evident on those to Vanbrugh's *Provok'd Husband* and Howard's *Committee*, but neither is dated.

One of the plays, Addison's *Cato*, 1730, differs entirely from the one he published in 1713 in that it contains the Poem to the Princess of Wales (1714), and 9 pages of 'Verses to the Author'. The latest dated play published in Johnson's lifetime appears thus far to be Lillo's *London Merchant*, 1731, it being the same date as the 1st edition; the latest play published by Scheurleer is Whitehead's *Roman Father*, with imprint 'London. Printed for R. Dodsley at Tully's head, Pall-mall; and sold by M. Cooper in Pater-noster Row, MDCCL'. This is the 2nd edition, though published in the same year as the 1st London edition. Apparently Johnson and his successors were executing work for the London booksellers from 1716 until 1750; a few examples of it have been located in the intervening period, but as the use of the extended alphabet in the process of printing is still evident in 1750, this peculiarity may solve some of the problems of indefinite or vague imprints, particularly with regard to anonymous or pirated publications. It has been noted that even Shakespeare's Fourth Folio, 1685, was being advertised as late as 1705, but it seems remarkable that some of Johnson's publications of 1710 should be a remainder in 1750, though this is by no means a record of suspended utilization.

Continued overleaf

Addenda and Corrigenda

ADDENDA

Page 77.   No. 63. This scarce second Hague edition, which was entirely reprinted, is remarkable for the inclusion of the fine prologue appreciating Shakespeare and Jonson commencing 'In country beauties', and for the omission of the four songs added to the edition of 1711. From information courteously given by Mr. Paul it appears that this prologue to Julius Caesar was first printed anonymously in Covent Garden Drollery 1672, the authorship was assigned to John Dryden by Bolton Corney in 1854, *N. & Q.*, and since then it has been included in several editions of Dryden's collected works. When Mr. Thorn-Drury had the Covent Garden Drollery reprinted in 1928 although he amply noted this prologue it seems he was unaware of its appearance in this Hague edition, which may be the only play in which it occurs.

CORRIGENDA

Page 9.   A large paper copy of the second issue is in a Philadelphia public library.

Page 39.   The 9th line from the bottom read after *published* 'c. 1709–10, the subtitles to'.

Page 49.   Printed by J. T. *should read* Printed by T. J.

Page 59.   N. C. Adler, Esq. *should read* E. N. Adler, Esq.

Page 62.   No. 8. There should be a rule after the Latin quotation as well as before it.   (*S.*)

Page 66.   No. 22. As the frontispiece is included in the alphabet, the pagination should be 30 pp. n.n. and (171) should read (169). This applies also to No. 23.

Page 68.   No. 27. MDCCXXIV *should read* MDCCXXXIV.

Page 104.   No. 165. 'Mackbet' *should read* 'Machbet', and the headline, p. 76, reads 'of Macbeth' instead of 'The Tragedy'.

Page 131.   No. 279. 24 pp. n.n. *should read* 22 pp. n.n.

Page 133.   No. 284. (*B.H.*) *should be omitted*.

Page 138.   No. 308. 120 *should read* (120).

Addenda and Corrigenda

ADDENDA

Page 104. No. 165. This scarce second Hague edition, which was entirely reprinted, is remarkable for the inclusion of the fine prologue appreciating Shakespeare and Jonson commencing 'In country beauties', and for the omission of the four songs added to the edition of 1711.

CORRIGENDA

Page 49.   Printed by J. T. *should read* Printed by T. J.

Page 59.   N. C. Adler, Esq. *should read* E. N. Adler, Esq.

Page 62.   No. 8. There should be a rule after the Latin quotation as well as before it.   (*S.*)

Page 66.   No. 22. As the frontispiece is included in the alphabet, the pagination should be 30 pp. n.n. and (171) should read (169). This applies also to No. 23.

Page 68.   No. 27. MDCCXXIV *should read* MDCCXXXIV.

Page 104.   No. 165. 'Mackbet' *should read* 'Machbet', and the headline, p. 76, reads 'of Macbeth' instead of 'The Tragedy'.

Page 131.   No. 279. 24 pp. n.n. *should read* 22 pp. n.n.

Page 133.   No. 285. (*B.H.*) *should be omitted.*

Page 138.   No. 308. 120 *should read* (120).

A COLLATION OF
THE SHAKESPEARE PLAYS
1700–1740
WITH SOME ACCOUNT OF
T. JOHNSON AND R. WALKER

My Books are all the Wealth I do possess,
And unto them I have engag'd my Heart.—T. L. C.

THE EDITIONS

ONLY the few can ever hope to add to their literary treasures a copy of either of the Folios, or the rarer first Quartos; but for those of antiquarian taste without the means of a Midas, there are the first octavo and smaller editions of the sets, and the many issues of the separately published plays printed in the early part of the eighteenth century still available. Admitting that the fine facsimiles of the Folios and Quartos may suffice for most, yet there is a charm attached to these early examples that one may seek for in vain elsewhere, and for those like-minded with ourselves as well as for those engaged on research, this description has been attempted.

By way of a preamble to enumerating and collating the many separate editions, with the adaptations, published from 1700 to 1740, a brief record of the complete editions from Rowe's to Theobald's has been found unavoidable, but in its inception this Love's Labour was not contemplated, although the recent discoveries in regard to Rowe's 1709 edition, and the finding of the erstwhile uncollated 1739 Dublin edition of Theobald's, may ensure that it is not lost.

Jacob Tonson, the doyen publisher of the Augustan

Age, merits some fitting recognition as the undoubted arouser of the public to an interest in these long-lying neglected but peerless dramas—an interest, as a ripple at first, that now washes the shores of the whole literary world. Nearly ninety years from the printing of the First Folio one may date an era in the evolution of our language caused by the study and assimilation of the philosophy and cadence of expression contained therein, the embodiment of the many proverbial quotations now part and parcel of our everyday speech, and the survival of a myriad of virile words that might meanwhile have perished from mere disuse.

One has only to attempt the reading of Father Chaucer, or even his great refiner Spenser, the Prince of Poets, to mark the gap that so divides theirs from these that furnish an eternal banquet of poesy and have now become our prose's melody.

The famous first octavo edition of the plays, described by Mr. Jackson in *The Library*, 1930, is here collated afresh largely owing to the recent discoveries of Dr. R. B. McKerrow (vide *Times Lit. Supplt.*, 8 March 1934). It was edited by Nicholas Rowe, laureated in 1715, but deceased three years later, and first published early in June 1709 by J. Tonson. It proved such a successful venture that a surreptitious reprint was made of it, and so closely was the original setting followed that for over 200 years the fact had evaded the scrutiny of bibliographers and Shakespearians alike, until Dr. McKerrow, the genial Secretary of the Bibliographical Society, made the important discovery that the text and title-pages had been entirely reprinted. There are several textual corrections and variations, but such lie outside the scope of the present article: some of Dr. McKerrow's first findings may be read in *The Times* essay. Fortunately, as I possessed a set of this reprint in its original state, the collation of it coinciding with that of Dr. McKerrow's is here given; it will enable those with sets to assign to which issue they belong and possibly lead to further interesting matter being disclosed. This reprinting was probably effected in 1710: it somewhat disjoints the sequence of the editions, the 'second edition', 1714, becoming now the third.

At this point I must record my appreciation of the kindly and considerable help willingly accorded me by Dr. McKerrow, and though he had started to assemble material for a similar undertaking, the master has relinquished the task to a prentice hand. Proud of his confidence I am, but fearsome of the path perilous with its pitfalls of detail, diction, and style.

It is unlikely that the exact date of the reprinting of this edition (really the second) can be ascertained except by inference; the fact was naturally a close secret of the publisher. One piece of negative evidence is extant in a copy of the first issue with the following on an original blank leaf preceding the frontispiece of vol. i: 'J: Bland: Oct. 1710. | Pr: Sheets:–1–1–6.' This was purchased at the dispersal of his library at Kippax Park, near Leeds, 1929, and appears to indicate that as late as 1710 sets of the first issue were still available, and there it must be left, until an ownership-dated copy of the second issue turns up.

Tonson, possibly taking into account the Shakespeare plays published at The Hague in 1710 which found their way here, and recognizing a further outlet for the sale of the works in a more convenient and less expensive form to a play-going and reading clientele, thereon produced a second edition in duodecimo in 1714. This was issued with at least three differing imprints in the successive order of publication. Complete sets of this edition are comparatively scarce, as against the earlier of 1709, and probably for this reason. In the large mansions in town and country the 1709 edition reposed in state in the library, but often the owners of these were again customers for the smaller and cheaper edition, either for their own use or for the amusement of the then large household staff attached to their residences: some copies do turn up marked specifically for 'The Housekeeper's Room'. Moreover, from the number of the separate plays that survive there appears to have been no greatly increased publication of them till several years later. Consequently, on the one hand, with a set of volumes convenient alike for the pocket and for acting purposes, and on the other an audience eager to read what they may have seen, volumes would be borrowed or taken with the best intentions, but, as many books do, would fail to find their way home.

In 1723–5 Tonson published Pope's first edition in 6 volumes, large quarto, supplemented with a like volume of the Poems. This was shortly followed by a well-printed issue of it in octavo, 8 volumes, by George Grierson, Dublin, 1726. Two years later, in 1728, Tonson published the second edition in duodecimo, 8 volumes, and this was supplemented with a ninth volume, and also issued again in 10 volumes, the tenth volume containing the Poems. The edition of Knapton's, 1731, tabulated by Lowndes, is probably erroneous. The last edition to be considered is that of Theobald in 7 volumes, post octavo, in 1733, again printed for Tonson but in conjunction with five other booksellers. This first text of Theobald's was again published, 1739, in Dublin, and is here described for the first time. A second edition followed, duodecimo, 8 volumes, in 1740, in which the notes are abridged.

Before embarking on the editions a word on the frontispieces may not be out of place. For many years it had been the custom in France to frontispiece their plays, and some of their best artists and most skilled engravers were employed thereat. One of the earliest examples of fine frontispiece work is evident in the plays of Corneille, published about 1664–6, yet until the early years of the eighteenth century there was no development here of any consequence in this direction. Few of those done for the plays during this period, until the coming of Gravelot, can vie with those of our neighbour. The following, in somewhat the order of their seniority, executed most of the Shakespeare frontispieces: M. Van der Gucht, E. Kirkall, L. Du Guernier, P. Foudrinier, J. Smith, G. King, Dandridge, and G. Van der Gucht after the charming designs of M. Gravelot. J. Clarke and J. Pine were occupied on similar work and may have done some of the unsigned plates.

In vol. ii, Rowe, 1709, there is a curious misdirection on the frontispiece to *Twelfth Night*, thus 'p. 719', which has caused it to be inserted in most copies at that page in *The Taming of the Shrew*. This is elucidated by the fact that in the first edition the last page of *All's Well* was misnumbered 718 instead of 818, and it also indicates that the plates were not numbered till after the works had been printed.

THE ARLAUD–DUCHANGE PORTRAIT

THE portrait of 'M^r: William Shakespear', 'B. Arlaud del.', 'G. Duchange scul.', sometimes found in vol. i of Rowe's 1709 edition, facing p. 1 of the 'Life' with directions at the bottom, 'p: 1: in the life' (*vide* British Museum copy), was not engraved till many years afterwards. Arlaud or Duchange are not known to have been in England prior to 1709: Duchange was attached to the Hanoverian Court, and probably did not visit here till 1714 or 1727. B. Arlaud, brother of the painter J. A. Arlaud, was certainly here prior to 1719, when he died, but the designer does not necessarily date the engraving, though it is very probable that Du Guernier engraved the small portrait in the 1714 edition of Rowe from Arlaud's drawing, as they are apparently derived from the same source. There is little actual data to work with: examples of book illustration bearing either of their names are scarce, as also is the portrait in question in its first state. It has never been considered otherwise than an extra illustration by

H. Arlaud del.   G. Duchange Sculp.

M͞r. W͞m. Shakespear

The first state of the Arlaud-Duchange portrait. There are rare
instances of its issue with the 1733 edition of Theobald's

B. Arlaud del.   G. Duchange Sculp.

$\mathcal{M}^{r}\ W^{m}\ Shakespeare$

The second state of the Arlaud-Duchange portrait, revealing the
alteration to the plate. Nearly all copies of the 1733 edition are with
the portrait thus

Mr. Wm. Shakespear

Lud. Du Guernier Sculp.

The portrait preceding the 'Life' in the 1714 edition.
Engraved from a painting or drawing similar to that
used for the 1733 edition of Theobald's

of both portraits somewhat clinches the matter. The watermark lines are identical, and they differ from those used in the 1709 edition.

As there is a difference of opinion whether this portrait was engraved and primarily issued about 1710 or in 1733, a further examination of the paper used in the two states of the engraving discloses that the wire lines in both of them are identical, and is therefore a reasonable indication that they were struck off about the same date. A comparison of the paper used for the frontispieces and the monument plate in the 1709 edition reveals that the wire lines are uniformly much closer together, and no trace of the wider form has been discovered in the whole issue. To elucidate the matter further the linage is depicted below.

The wire lines in the paper of both portraits 1st and 2nd state 1733.

1733	1733	1733
1709	1709	1709

The wire lines in the paper of the monument plate and others 1709.

The Shakespeare Portraits in the 1709, 1714, 1728, and 1733 editions

Shakespeare's portrait by M. Van der Gucht, in oval, forming the frontispiece to vol. i, Rowe's 1709 edition, may possibly have been adapted from the *Droeshout*. The costume is on the same lines, though the collar is entirely different, having strings as shown in the *Chandos*, and it faces to the left as both originals do. To the edition of *1714* a portrait was added by Lud. Du Guernier to face 'p 1. in ye Life', still *facing to the left*, but the features and costume are entirely different. There are no strings to the collar, and the undercoat is unbuttoned to the seventh button, revealing the shirt and collar as being of one piece. A smaller replica of this portrait forms the centre of the frontispiece to vol. i. It was afterwards used for Pope's second edition of 1728 and in a very worn state for the collections of Tonson and Walker of 1734–5.

In 1733 this same Du Guernier portrait reappears in a larger state, engraved by G. Duchange from a drawing by B. Arlaud, only in *this case it faces to the right*, the only noticeable difference being that the ear-ring which had been previously omitted reappears. The attire does not correspond with the Chandos as we now know it, and it seems possible there may have been then extant another portrait of Shakespeare, of which we now have no trace, as the source of these engravings.

The lineaments and costume of the 1714 and 1733 engravings are so similar as to suggest a common source for the two engravings, but if Arlaud drew the portrait for the 1714 engraving by Du Guernier, why was it engraved facing the other way by Duchange for the 1733 edition?

Arlaud is supposed to have died in England in 1719, and the Chandos portrait was in the possession of Mr. Keck till 1725. Wivell suggested in 1827 that Arlaud had drawn his portrait from the Chandos, but that he had nearly omitted the beard.

Mr. G. E. Dawson, of The Folger Shakespeare Library, has kindly intimated that he has a forthcoming article on this subject in *The Library*, which may throw more light on this problem.

ABBREVIATIONS

To condense the descriptions as far as possible and also define the collations, the following abbreviations, &c., are used: All words or dates underlined thus are printed in red.

> The terms 4to, 8vo, 12mo refer to the gathering of the leaves respectively in fours, eights, and twelves, and any departure is noted.
>
> The pagination gives the actual number; brackets are used when the figures are not printed (1).
>
> n. = numbered; n.n. = not numbered; pn. = pagina-

tion; F. = Frontispiece; V. = Volume; G.T. =
General Title; V.T. = Volume Title; P.T. = Play
Title; a rule is signified thus | = | and a double
rule | ≡ | ; O. = Printer's ornament; Hp. and Tp.
= head- and tail-pieces respectively.

Any further abbreviations used for the separate plays
will be found in that section (pp. 58–60).

SHAKESPEAR, 1709

THE first edition of what is commonly known as Rowe's
was printed and published about midsummer 1709, in
8vo, 6 volumes, a portion being printed on large paper.
Previous to this date a complete set of the plays was only
available in the Folios of 1623, 1632, 1663–4, and 1685.

The ordinary edition averages in size $4\frac{5}{8}'' \times 7\frac{5}{8}''$; one-
eighth of an inch larger each way would be the outside
limit unless uncut, and there seems to be no example
in that state known. Large paper copies (royal 8vo)
appear to be confined to the first edition. The portrait
frontispiece by M. Van der Gucht is often found gracing
every volume, but such is not essential to a complete
set, although it is to the first volume. A few copies,
probably not more than half a dozen, of the large paper
edition were published so as to be bound up 'in nine
volumes'. At South Kensington the Dyce copy is an
example of the 9 volume set further enlarged to 11
volumes through the Poems being bound up in two
parts: it has the Arlaud-Duchange portrait inserted
insititiously. The general title and volume titles were
printed so, and the contents were adapted to the lesser
number of plays comprised in each volume, but the text
remained unaltered; in these *de luxe* sets there is a portrait to each of the 9 volumes. At the dispersal of the
Duke of Leeds's Library at Sotheby's in June 1930
there was a copy. Sets in contemporary binding in
untouched state are scarce. Some are plain with blind-
tooled sides, others have the backs heavily decorated in
gold, the acorn pattern being popular.

ROWE'S SHAKESPEAR, FIRST ISSUE

General Title. Vol. I. The| Works| of| Mr. William Shakespear;| in| Six Volumes| =| Adorn'd with Cuts. | =| Revis'd and Corrected, with an Account of| the Life and Writings of the Author.| By N. Rowe, Esq; | =| London:| Printed for Jacob Tonson, within Grays-Inn| Gate, next Grays-Inn Lane. MDCCIX.

6 vols. 8vo. This and the other 5 volumes contain a volume title with imprint. 'London:| Printed for Jacob Tonson, at Grays-Inn| Gate. MDCCIX', enumerating the contents. There should be an engraved frontispiece portrait to vol. i and a plate of the Stratford monument at p. 37 in the 'Life', and a frontispiece to each play. These titles and plates are not included in the alphabets or pagination except vol. vi, in which the title is A2.

Collation. Vol. I, 8vo. G.T. and V.T. 2 ll. A–A⁴, a–b⁸, c⁴, B–Z, Aa–Gg. pn. 12 n.n.+(i)–xl. (xxviii numbered xviii)+(1)–(464), of which 143 n. 127, and 232 n. 326. Headlines to pp. 415, 429, 445. 'Labours', dramatis personae (Bᵛ), 'Boat-Swain' thus.

Vol. II. V.T. 1 l. B–Kk. pn. (465)–(976), of which 726 n. 716; 818 n. 718; 942 n. 642; 970 n. 670.

Vol. III. V.T. 1 l. B–Nn. pn. (977)–(1536), of which 1245 n. 1248; 1247 n. 2247; 1261 n. 2261; 1338 n. 1331; 1339 n. 1330; 1454 n. 1455; 1455 n. 1454. The headline p. 1059 'King Richard'. (Q4) initial 'O' upside down.

Vol. IV. V.T. 1 l. B–Mm⁴. pn. (1537)–2072, of which 1751 n. 175; 2044 n. 044. Headline, p. 2001, reads 'Titus Andronicus'. In the alphabet (T2) is not printed and 'Drammatis' is so.

Vol. V. V.T. 1 l. B–Oo. pn. (2073)–(2648), of which 2102 n. 3102; 2103 n. 3103; 2192 n. 1192; 2302 n. 3302; 2303 n. 3303; 2306 n. 3306; 2307 n. 3307; 2310 n. 3311; 2311 n. 3312; 2558 n. 2556; 2559 n. 2557; 2562 n. 2560; 2563 n. 2561; 2566 n. 2564; 2567 n. 2565.

Vol. VI. A–Nn. pn. (2649)–3324, the only blank leaf in the set being A1, pp. (2649–50), of which 2757 n. 2765; 2788 n. 2688; 2789 n. 2689; 2900 n. 3000; 2901 n. 3001; 2904 to 2920 n. 3004 to 3020; 2937 n. 3037, whence the pagination continues to 3324 (eliding 100 pp.), of which 3124 n. 3224. The headline, p. 3110, 'The Life and Death, &c.'

ROWE'S SHAKESPEAR, SECOND ISSUE
(actually Second Edition)

Collation and description taken from the 'Preston' copy now in the Folger Shakespeare Library, and also collated with Dr. McKerrow's copy (6 vols., 8vo, 1709). Signatures of original owner, Sir Nath. Preston, p. 979, and descendants, W.andN. Preston, volume title, vol. v.

The size, type, alphabets, total number of pages, and frontispieces to all intents correspond with the first edition. Most of the pagination errors were rectified, but are replaced by as many fresh ones. The easily discernible variants in important pages are for the most part here described. Neither frontispieces, general title, nor volume titles are included in the alphabets or pagination except vol. vi, where a blank leaf and volume title are (A1 and 2). The text variants correspond with Dr. McKerrow's article. The portrait and play frontispieces are identical in both editions.

Vol. I. 8vo. The G.T. and V.T. two leaves+A4, a–c4, B–Z, Aa–Gg. pn. the first 12 n.n. (i)–xl, (1)–(464).

Imprint of G.T.: the 'a' of 'Lane' is not in a direct line with the comma after 'Tonson'. V.T.: the 'V' of 'Verona' is in a line with the 'T' of 'Two'. Dedication (A) is without the armorial Hp. Dramatis personae (Bᵛ), 'Boat-fwain' thus; and p. xxviii numbered so.

Errors in pn.: 48 n. 16; 55 n. 53; 134 n. 314; 175 n. 171; 185 n. 181.

Vol. II. V.T. one leaf+B–Kk. pn. (465)–(976), the first leaf n.n.

Imprint of V.T.: the 'M' of date is in a line with the 'T' of 'Tonson'. (B2): the initial 'N' is upside down. P.T. (T3): the 'S' of 'All's Well' is out of line (i.e. in centre).

Errors in pn.: 527 n. 727; 714 n. 174; 774 n. 757; 846 n. 826; 847 n. 827; 901 n. 991. Note 714 is corrected in McKerrow's and another copy.

Vol. III. V.T. one leaf+B–Nn. pn. (977)–(1536), the first leaf n.n.

Imprint of V.T.: the numerals to the Henry's V, VI, VII are in line. (Q4): the initial 'O' is the right way up. (X5ᵛ): the absence of four larger dots to Tp. P.T. (Dd): the stop after 'VI' is in line. Headline (G2) correct.

Errors in pn.: 1183 n. 1184; 1247 n. 2247; 1259 n. 2259; 1261 n. 2261; 1454 n. 1455; 1455 n. 1454.

Vol. IV. V.T. one leaf+B–Mm⁴. pn. (1537)–2072, the first leaf n.n.

Imprint of V.T.: the word 'at' is slightly to the right of the 'X' of date. Hp. (G2): the repeating ornament is lateral instead of vertical, and this applies to ornament P.T. (T). 'T2' is printed and 'Dramatis' so. P.T. (Bb) and (Hh2): the stop to 'Tragedy' is in line, and the headline (Hh) is correct. The ornament of Hp. (Hh3) is divided in the centre.

Errors in pn.: 1566 n. 1567; 1567 n. 1585; 1597 n. 1567; 1993 n. 1963; 1998 n. 998.

Vol. V. V.T. one leaf+B–Oo. pn. (2073)–(2648), the first leaf n.n.

Imprint of V.T.: the 'S' of 'Athens' is in a line with the stop after 'Juliet'. P.T. (B): the stop to 'Tragedy' is in line. Hp. (U4) ornament has divisional dots. Tp. (Hh8): the ornament is lateral instead of vertical, and P.T. (Ii) there is no stop to 'Tragedy'.

Errors in pn.: 2439 n. 2436; 2466 n. 1466; 2494 n. 2594; 2519 n. 2419; 2556 to 2568 n. 2554 to 2566. This series is worse in the 1st edition.

Vol. VI. A–Nn. pn. (2649)–3324.

Imprint of V.T.: the 'C' of 'Containing' lines with the 'L' of 'volume'. P.T. (A3): the 'The' of imprint nearly centres with ornament. P.T. (G2): the stop to 'Tragedy' is only slightly raised, and that to 'Comedy' P.T. (R3) is in line. Hp.: Cupid block is cracked (R4). The division in Hp. (U7) is nearly in the centre. Headline (Z5ᵛ) lacks '&c.'. Trefoil instead of acorn ornament P.T. (Ee2), and the stops to 'Puritan' are towards the centre.

Errors in pn.: 2664 n. 2964; 2667 n. 2697; 2701 n. 2852; 2757 n. 2767; 2885 n. 2685, 2905 to 2920 n. 3005 to 3020; 2937 n. 3037, whence the paging continues (eliding 100 pp.) to 3324, in which 3209 n. 3299. A1 (p. 2649–50) is the only blank leaf in the set. Mispaging in the first edition commences on 2904.

In 1710 a supplementary volume was published containing the Poems, &c., as follows. Though it is designated 'Volume the Seventh' it does not belong to the edition, though with it a set is esteemed the more.

Collation. The| Works| of| Mr. William Shakespear. Volume the Seventh.| Containing,|

Venus & Adonis.| Tarquin & Lucrece| And| His Miscellany| Poems.| With Critical Remarks| on his Plays, &c. to| which is Prefix'd an| Essay on the Art, Rise| and Progress of the| Stage in Greece, Rome | and England.

THE
WORKS

OF

Mr. *William Shakespear*;

IN

SIX VOLUMES.

ADORN'D with CUTS.

Revis'd and Corrected, with an Account of
the Life and Writings of the Author.
By *N. ROWE*, Efq;

L O N D O N:

Printed for *Jacob Tonfon*, within *Grays-Inn*
Gate, next *Grays-Inn* Lane. MDCCIX.

The General Title to volume i published with the
reprinted 1709 edition. Note that in the first edition the
first 'C' of the date lies under the 'G' of 'Grays-Inn'.

London: | Printed for E. Curll at the Dial and Bible |
against St. Dunstan's Church, and E. Sanger | at the
Post-House at the Middle-Temple Gate. | MDCCX.

8vo. A, a–e⁴, A–Gg⁷. pn. 16 pp. n.n.+i–lxxii+(1)–(478). 104 n.
16; 225 n. 125; 228 n. 128; 229 n. 129; 302 n. 300, this was corrected in some and in the l.p. 461 n. 361.

There is an inserted leaf n.n. between (48) and (49)
and a plate of Venus and Adonis preceding the title to
it. This latter with the Lucrece title are dated 1709.
The dedication is signed 'S.N.', being the terminal
letters of Charles Gildon, and the last leaf has an advertisement, 'Books Printed for E Curll and E Sanger'.
A few of this volume were also printed on better and
in large paper.

ROWE'S SECOND EDITION
(*actually the Third*)

THIS, ostensibly the second edition, was published in
12mo, in 8 and 9 volumes, 1714, and was issued with
three differing general title-pages, twice in 8 volumes,
and once in 9 volumes. The text in the first 8 volumes
of each appears to be identical. Each volume commences with a fresh pagination and consequently the
initial plays have sometimes been described as separate
entities, whereas unless the title-pages differ from those
in this edition, they must be considered as excerpts. It
has been stated that any new features to this edition
'were not the work of Rowe himself', but this is con-
trary to the statement made on the general titles to the
two issues in 8 volumes. An engraved frontispiece
portrait by Du Guernier faces the title to volume i. The
framing is nearly a close copy of that done by Van der
Gucht for the 1709 edition, but the portrait is in minia-
ture of the larger one done by Du Guernier, 'p 1 in
yᵉ Life'. This portrait was again engraved in reverse by
Duchange for Theobald's edition, 1733.

A woodcut laureated oval portrait ornaments each
volume title. The Duke of Somerset's arms in woodcut

heads the dedication; and the 'Life' is nearly a reprint word for word of the first edition, but the monument plate in a smaller size is more crudely executed. The play frontispieces, although depicting most of the same incidents, were nearly all engraved from fresh drawings with the characters more in keeping with their period, but the episodes depicted in the following differ entirely: *The Tempest, The Merry Wives of Windsor, Richard II, Cymbeline,* and *The Puritan.*

Many of the plates not signed by Du Guernier were engraved by Kirkall. The index, which is placed at the end of vol. viii, was probably done by Mr. Hughes, to whom Tonson paid £28 7s. 0d., and this possibly included a supervision of the text in its smaller size. It is interesting to note that Curll was advertising the 9-volume edition at £1 7s. 10d. in 1715 and Bettesworth similarly at £1 7s. There is a contents title following each volume title, and they are included in the alphabet and pagination, but the frontispieces to the plays are not. The volume titles all bear the imprint 'London: | Printed for Jacob Tonson in the Strand. | MDCCXIV.' and the play titles 'Printed in the Year MDCCXIV.' The full size of an uncut copy would be $4\frac{1}{8}'' \times 7''$; the average size of a bound copy is $3\frac{3}{4}'' \times 6\frac{3}{8}''$.

Collation. Rowe's 1714 edition, 12mo, 8 and 9 volumes

The general title-pages of the three issues in the order of their publication, the first being a very scarce imprint:

(1) The Works | of | Mr. William Shakespear; | in | Eight volumes. | = | Adorn'd with Cutts. | = | Revis'd and Corrected, with an Account of | The Life and Writings of the Author, | By N. Rowe, Esq; | = | London: | Printed for Jacob Tonson at Shakespear's- | Head over-against Catherine-Street in the Strand. | MDCCXIV.

(N.B. No mention of the index, although issued in vol. viii.)

(2) The | Works | of | Mr. William Shakespear; | in |

Eight Volumes.| = Adorn'd with Cutts.| =| Revis'd and Corrected, with an Account of | The Life and Writings of the Author, | By N. Rowe, Esq;| =| To this Edition is added, A Table of the| most Sublime Passages in this Author. | =| London, | Printed for J. Tonson: And are to be Sold by J. Knapton| and D. Midwinter in St. Paul's Church-yard, A Betsworth| on London-Bridge, W. Taylor in Pater-noster Row, T, Varnam | and J. Osborn in Lombard-street, and J. Browne near| Temple-Bar. MDCCXIV.

(3) The| Works| of| Mr. William Shakespear, | in| Nine Volumes:| with his Life, by N. Rowe Esq;| =| Adorn'd with Cuts.| =| To the last Volume is prefix'd | I. An Essay | on the Art, Rise, and Progress of the | Stage, in Greece, Rome, and England. | II. Observations upon the most Sublime| Passages in this Author. III. A Glossary, | explaining the Antiquated Words made | use of throughout his Works, | =| London, | Printed for J. Tonson, E. Curll, I. Pemberton, and K.| Sanger: And are to be Sold by J. Knapton and D.| Midwinter in St Paul's Church-yard, A. Betsworth on London-Bridg, [*sic*] W. Taylor in Pater-noster-Row, T. Var- | nam and J. Osborn in Lombard-street and J. Browne| near Temple-Bar. MDCCXIV.

N.B. The versos of (1) and (2) are blank, but on (3) the following is printed, 'The Inscription upon Mr Shake-| spear's Monument, omitted in his Life, | Stay Passenger, why goest thou by soe fast?| Read, if thou canst whom envious Death hath plac'd | Within this monument: Shakespear, with whome | Quick Nature dy'd: whose Name doth deck the Tombe | Far more than Cost, sith all that he hath writ| Leaves living Art but Page to serve his Wit.' The spelling on the monument differs from this.

Collation. Vol. I. 12mo. A, a, b⁶, B–S. pn. 10 ll. n.n. (i)–xl+(1)–(408). The portrait frontispiece is A, and S 11 and 12 are blank leaves. The preliminary leaves consist of F., G.T., V.T., contents T., dedication 6 ll., and the 'Life', xl pp. There is a frontispiece to each play in

THE
WORKS
OF
Mr. *William Shakespear* ;
IN
EIGHT VOLUMES.

ADORN'D with CUTTS.

Revis'd and Corrected, with an Account of
the Life and Writings of the Author,
By *N. ROWE*, Efq;

LONDON:
Printed for JACOB TONSON at *Shakefpear's-
Head* ovei-againft *Catherine-Street* in the *Strand.*
MDCCXIV.

The General Title to the first issue of Rowe's second
edition, in which he is credited with its revision and
correction.

every volume, and these with the portrait and monument plate in vol. i are not in the alphabet or pagination. p. 84 n. 94.

Vol. II. A–T⁶. pn. (1)–(444), p. 289 n. 389.

Vol. III. A–R⁶. pn. (1)–(396), of which 55 n. 24; 58 n. 34; 59 n. 93; 133 n. 113; 136 n. 316.

Vol. IV. A–S. pn. (1)–(432), of which 202 n. 200; 203 n. 201; 206 n. 204; 207 n. 205; 210 n. 208; 211 n. 209; 214 n. 212; 215 n. 213; 256 n. 259; 354 n. 345; 395 n. 295.

Vol. V. B–U⁶. pn. (1)–(468), of which 60 n. 69; 362 n. 338; 363 n. 339; 366 n. 342; 367 n. 343; 370 n. 346; 371 n. 347; 374 n. 350; 375 n. 351; 378 n. 354; 379 n. 355; 382 n. 358; 383 n. 359; in some copies 142 n. 442; and 143 n. 443.

Vol. VI. A–R. pn. (1)–(408), of which 57 n. 75; 180 n. 189; 181 n. 188; 237 n. 337; 256 n. 526, the last leaf being blank.

Vol. VII. A–Q. pn. (1)–384, of which 322 n. 320; 323 n. 321; 326 n. 324; 327 n. 325; 330 n. 328; 331 n. 329; 334 n. 342; 335 n. 343.

Vol. VIII. A–S⁶. pn. (1)–(420); of these the last 23 pp. are n.n., but 122 n. 98; 123 n. 99; 130 n. 102; 131 n. 103; 134 n. 106; 135 n. 107; 138 n. 110; 139 n. 111; 142 n. 114; 143 n. 115; 151 n. 150; 192 n. 190; 230 n. 330; 397 n. 39; in some copies 151 corrected. p. 398 (39) states in the three issues 'The End of the Eighth and Last Volume'. The headline, p. 247, reads 'Odcastle'.

The title of vol. ix reads thus:

The| Works| of| Mr. William Shakespear.| Volume the Ninth.| =| [O. an intertwined monogrammic J.D.] | =| London, | Printed by J. Darby in Bartholomew-Close, for E. Curll,| K. Sanger, and J. Pemberton: Sold by J. Tonson in | the Strand, J. Knapton and D. Midwinter in St. Paul's | Church-yard, A. Betsworth on London Bridg, W. Taylor | in Pater-noster-Row, N. Cliff and D. Jackson near the| Poultry, T. Varnam and J. Osborn in Lombard-street, | and J. Browne near Temple-Bar. M.DCC.XIV.

It contains a 'Venus and Adonis' and a 'Tarquin and Lucrece' plate both by M. Van der Gucht, with an extra leaf preceding p. 45, and these with the volume title and contents title are not in the alphabet or pagination.

Collation. 2 ll.+a–c⁴, B–S. pn. 2 ll. n.n.+i–lvi+(1)–408. S12 is probably the inserted leaf at p. 45, and is so reckoned, the last numbered page being 406.

POPE'S FIRST EDITION

THE ambitious edition of Alexander Pope was published in 1723–5, in 6 volumes, large 4to, at £6 6s. per set and largely by subscription. It was well printed on good paper and practically without pagination errors. Volume i contains the Shakespeare portrait engraved by G. Vertue, 1721, after the Harley painting, and an engraving of the Stratford monument also by him, but considerably differing from that depicted previously. Doubts have been raised as to whether the present bust is the identical one placed there anterior to 1623. It was first engraved for Dugdale's *Warwickshire*, 1656. Betterton, the actor, visited Stratford to gain any available information for the 'Life' that Rowe wrote; assuming that he saw the tomb, it is likely that if the monument appeared then much different from the engraving, Rowe would have been acquainted with the fact, and the illustrations in the editions of 1709 and 1714 would not have been based on the Dugdale engraving. Another engraving was executed by Vertue for Pope's 1725 edition, and re-engraved by Fourdrinier for the smaller edition of 1728. These depict very marked differences in the lineaments of the bard as well as in the architectural details of the monument, and neither of them accords with the monument as it now is. In common with many of the monuments of that period it was coloured, and sculptured with that end in view. It may or may not have been touched during the troublous times of the Commonwealth, but play-actors may have equally suffered with saints. There are records of some restoration immediately prior to the Stratford Jubilee, inaugurated by Garrick in 1769, and under the direction of Malone in 1793 the then faded colouring was partly removed and it was whitened, to be again cleaned and the colouring restored as far as it was traceable in 1861. This monumental question has been dealt with exhaustively by M. H. Spielmann in *The Title-Page of the First*

Folio—to the disparagement of the engravers and the fair fame of Stratford's pride.

The collation is as follows:

Vol. I. *General Title*. The| Works| of| Shakespear. | in | Six Volumes. | = | Collated and Corrected by the former Editions, | By Mr. Pope | = | —Laniatum corpore toto [&c., 6 lines]. Virg. | = | London : | Printed for Jacob Tonson in the Strand. | = | MDCCXXV.

This volume should have a portrait after the Harley painting, and an engraving of the Stratford monument by G. Vertue, dated 1721. The second title to vol. i reads : 'The Works | of | Mr. William Shakespear. | = | Volume the First. | Consisting of | Comedies. | = | London : | Printed for Jacob Tonson in the Strand. | = | MDCCXXIII.' It is printed in black, and the volume titles II to VI are similar except for the variation of the volume number and the contents. The versos of all these titles are printed thus, 'Plays contain'd in this Volume', and are here given in an abbreviated form with the collations; also, to avoid repetition, the play position in the 7 volumes of Theobald's 1733 edition is given in brackets thus, Tempest (1·1) indicating the first play in vol. 1.

Vol. I. 'Comedies.' Tempest (1·1), M. Night's D. (1·2), Two Gentlemen (1·3), Merry Wives (1·4), Measure for M. (1·5), Much Ado (1·6).

4to. A, a–f, B–Cccc². pn. 2 pp. n.n.+[i]–xli+13 pp. n.n.+ (1)–(564).

Vol. II. 'Comedies.' M. of Venice (2·1), L. L. Lost (2·2), As You Like It (2·3), The Shrew (2·4), All 's Well (2·5), Twelfth N. (2·6), Winter's T. (3·2).

4to. A–Nnnn. pn. (1)–656.

Vol. III. 'Historical Plays.' K. Lear (5·2), K. John (3·3), Rich. II (3·4), Henry IV, Pt. I (3·5), and Pt. II (3·6), Henry V (4·1).

4to. A–Cc, M–Rrr². pn. 4 pp. n.n.+(1)–(204) of which 85– 203 are bracketed, +89–(500).

Vol. IV. 'Historical Plays.' Henry VI, Pt. I (4·2), Pt. II (4·3), Pt. III (4·4), Rich. III (4·5), Henry VIII (5·1).

4to. A–Zzz². pn. (1)–(548).

Vol. V. 'Tragedies from History.' Timon (5·4), Coriolanus (6·1), J. Caesar (6·2), Antony and C. (6·3), Titus A. (5·5), Macbeth (5·3).

4to. A–Ffff. pn. (1)–(600).

Vol. VI. 'Tragedies from Fable.' Troilus (7·1), Cymbeline (6·4), Romeo (7·2), Hamlet (7·3), Othello (7·4).

4to. A–Eeee. Ffff–Oooo in twos. pn. (1)–(592)+36 n.n.

A Vol. VII accompanied it as follows:

The| Works| of Mr. William Shakespear.| =| The Seventh Volume.| =| Containing| Venus and Adonis. |Tarquin and Lucrece.| || |And Mr. Shakespear's Mis-| cellany Poems. | To which is Prefix'd, | An Essay on the Art, Rise, and Progress of| the Stage, in Greece, Rome, and England.| And a Glossary of the Old Words us'd in these Works. | = | The Whole Revis'd and Corrected with a Preface, | By Dr. Sewell.| =| Lon- don; | Printed by J. Darby, for A. Bettesworth, F. Fayram, | W. Mears, J. Pemberton, J. Hooke, C. Rivington,| F. Clay, J. Batley, E. Symon. M.DCC.XXV.

A, a, a–Mmm. pn. (i)–(xvi)+i–(lviii)+(1)–iv, (5)[*sic*]–44+(1)– 66, +(177)[*sic*]–(456). aʳ and bʳ have misprint 'Vol. VIII'. The last 2 pages contain 'The Table'. The essay was the work of C. Gildon.

(B.M., B.H.)

POPE'S FIRST EDITION (DUBLIN)

FOLLOWING nearly immediately this sumptuous edition, an 8vo set in 8 volumes was published in Dublin, pos- sibly unauthorized. The title to vol. i as follows:

The| Works| of | Shakespear.| =| in eight volumes. | =| Collated and Corrected by the | former Editions, | By Mr. Pope.| =| Laniatum corpore [&c., 6 lines]. Virg.|

= |Dublin :| Printed by and for Geo. Grierson,| in Essex-Street, and for George | Ewing, in Dames-Street. | = | MDCCXXVI.

8vo. ‡I, A, B4, C, d4, eI, C–F, GI, H–Z, Aa–Ff4. pn. 13 pp. n.n.+ i–xxiii, 3 pp. n.n.+1–(410). The 13 pp. include two titles, Preface, and Subscribers, n.n.; then i–xxiii, containing the 'Life', and 3 pp. n.n. containing B. Jonson's poem and 'The Tempest' title dated MDCCXXV (1)– (66). 'A Midsummer-Nights | Dream' has also a similarly dated title (67)–128, and from thence continuous pn. to (410), the last 2 pp. being 'Books Printed'. All other P.T. are only half-titles. The second G.T. is printed wholly in black, omitting 'in eight volumes', and dated MDCCXXV.

Each of the succeeding volume titles is printed in red and black and dated MDCCXXVI and they are not included in the alphabet or pagination.

Vol. II. The| Works| of| Shakespear.| =| Volume the Second.| =| Consisting of| Comedies,| viz.| Much Ado |about | Nothing. | [etc.] | Dublin: Printed by and for George Grierson, | at the Two Bibles in Essex-Street, and for, | George Ewing, at the Angel and | Bible in Dames-Street. | = | MDCCXXVI.

8vo. ‡I, A–Gg4. pn. 2 pp. n.n.+(1)–(472).
The imprints to vol. vi and to the second title in vol. i read similarly to this.
The imprints to vols. iii, iv, v, vii, and viii read similarly to the G.T. vol. i with a slight variation in spacing.

Vol. III. The| Works| of| Shakespear.| =| Volume the Third. | =| Consisting of Comedies and Historical Plays,| viz.| Twelfth Night [&c.]—| Dublin:

8vo. A–Ee4. pn. 4 pp. n.n.+(1)–438.

Vol. IV. *ut supra*. 'Consisting of| Historical Plays,| viz. King Henry IV. Part I [&c.]—|

8vo. 1 leaf+A–Ff². pn. 2 pp. n.n.+(1)–452.

Vol. V. 'Consisting of | Historical Plays and Trage-dies |from History'. | viz. | King Henry VI. Part III | [&c.]

8vo. 1 leaf+A–Ff. pn. 2 pp. n.n.+(1)–464.

Vol. VI. 'Consisting of | Tragedies from History | and Tragedies from Fable'. | viz. | Julius Caesar. | [&c.]

8vo. 1 leaf+A–Ee⁴. pn. 2 pp. n.n.+(1)–440.

Vol. VII. 'Consisting of | Tragedies from Fable'. | viz. | Cymbeline | [&c.]

8vo. 1 leaf+‡1+A–Dd⁴ ∴⁸, C–G in fours. pn. 2 pp. n.n.+(1)– 424+56 pp. n.n. including advertisement leaf.

Vol. VIII. The Works | of Shakespear. | = | Volume the Eighth, | = | containing | Venus and Adonis. | Tar-quin and Lucrece. | And Mr. Shakespear's Miscellany Poems. | To which is Prefix'd | An Essay on the Art, Rise, and Pro- | gress of the Stage, in Greece, Rome, and England. | And a Glossary of the Old Words us'd in these | Works. | = | The whole Revis'd and Corrected with a Preface, | By Dr. Sewell. | = | Dublin: | Printed by and for George Grierson, in Essex-Street, and for George Ewing in | Dames-Street | = | MDCCXXVI.

8vo. ‡1, A–Gg. pn. title, 2 pp. n.n.+(i)–(xii)+1–(468). In the 'Books Printed', the last leaf, Grierson and Ewing advertise *Hamlet*, *Julius Caesar*, and *Othello* (q.v. 48, 70, and 219.) (*B.M., B.H.*)

POPE'S SECOND EDITION

Pope's second edition was published in 1728, with varying imprints, in 8, 9, and 10 volumes. 12mo.

The set was first issued as follows:

Vol. I. The | Works | of | Shakespear. | in | Eight Volumes. | = | Collated and Corrected by the former Editions, | By Mr. Pope. | = | The Second Edition. | = | [six lines of Latin verse by Virgil, commencing 'Laniatum corpore toto'] | = | London: | Printed for J. Tonson in the Strand. | = | MDCCXXVIII.

12mo. A–C⁶, D–T. pn. F. and G.T. 4 pp. n.n.+(i)–lii+5 pp. n.n. +(1)–(384). pp. xxvi–xxx are n.n., xxxi the number is misplaced to the inner corner, 27 n. 25; 232 n. 32; 249 n. 449; 326 n. 26, though corrected in some.

There is a monument plate by Fourdrinier facing

p. xxxviii, with a frontispiece by either L. Du Guernier or Fourdrinier to each play, and neither is included in the collation or pagination in this or the other volumes. Each has a volume title, 'The | Works | of Shakespear. | = | Volume . . . | = | [O. Shakespeare's head in oval] | = | London : | Printed for J. Tonson in the Strand. | = | MDCCXXVIII'. On the verso is the contents, and to each play is a half-title with only the title of the play between rules.

Vol. II. A–Q. pn. (1)–384, of which 88 n. 81; 146 n. 156; 147 n. 59; 150 n. 154; 151 n. 149; 331 n. 321.

Vol. III. A–T. pn. (1)–(456), the last 2 pp. being blank and 137 n. 147.

Vol. IV. A–U. pn. (1)–480, the last 4 pp. being blank.

Through a misdirection on the frontispiece to *Henry IV*, Part I, it may be bound up at p. 87, and this volume sometimes has the imprint as described to vol. v. In some copies, but very rarely, the tail-piece to p. 85 is a banner with head aureated.

Vol. V. A–R. pn. (1)–408.

The imprint is as follows in all copies : London : Printed for J. Tonson in the Strand ; | and for J. Darby, A. Bettes- | worth, and F. Clay, in Trust for | Richard, James, and Bethel | Wellington. | = | MDCCXXVIII.

Vol. VI. A–P. pn. (1)–360.

Vol. VII. A–Q⁶. pn. (1)–(372), 53 n. 35.

Vol. VIII. A–S, then T–Aa in sixes. pn. (1)–(428)+76 pp. n.n. containing index and various readings, the last leaf being a blank. The pn. runs (1)–144, 245–315, 216–(428). In all cases, whether to the 8th, 9th, or 10th volume edition, p. 427 reads, 'The end of Shakespear's Plays'.

Very shortly afterwards, and in the same year, 'Volume the Ninth' was issued, bearing the same imprint as vol. v, but spaced differently, and containing the apocryphal plays of *Pericles*, &c., in the same order as in Rowe's edition, 1714, vol. viii. Pope ignored these plays in the first edition, and the text of these is practically a reprint of Rowe's edition. This volume owes its existence to the demands of the public or booksellers. Whether found as an addition to the 8-volume set or in the 9 volumes as advertised or the 10-volume set, there appears to be no difference, and every volume ends with (p. 426) 'The End of the Ninth and Last Volume'.

Collation. 12mo. A–S. pn. (1)–(432), the last 6 pp. being advertisements, 'Books printed for Jacob Tonson' and the other partners. The contents title is on A2, and the P.Ts. have each a printer's ornament and 'Printed in the Year MDCCXXVIII'.

Bearing the same date, the 10-volume set was issued with title to vol. i. 'The | Works | of | Mr. William Shakespear. | In Ten Volumes. | = | Publish'd by Mr. Pope and Dr. Sewell. | = | [O. decorated vase of fruit.] | = | London: | Printed for J. and J. Knapton, J. Darby, A. Bet- | tesworth, J. Tonson, F. Fayram, W. Mears, | J. Pemberton, J. Osborn and T. Longman, | B. Motte, C. Rivington, F. Clay, J. Batley, | Ri. Ja. and B. Wellington. 1728.

Except for this title, the contents of this and the next 8 volumes are exactly as heretofore recorded, with the addition of this volume.

The | Works | of | Mr. William Shakespear. | = | The Tenth Volume. | = | containing | Venus and Adonis. | Tarquin and Lucrece. | with | His Miscellany Poems. | To which are added, | Critical Remarks on his Plays, | And an Essay on the Art, Rise, and | Progress of the Stage, in Greece, Rome, | and England. Both by Mr. Gildon. | Also a Glossary of the Old Words us'd in | these Works. | = | The Whole Revis'd and Corrected, with a Preface, | By Dr. Sewell. | = | London: | Printed for J. and J. Knapton, J. Darby, A. Bettes- | worth, F. Fayram, W. Mears, J. Pemberton, | J. Osborn and T. Longman, B. Motte, J. Hooke, | C. Rivington, F. Clay, and J. Batley. 1728.

12mo. A⁶, B–U. pn. (1)–xii+(1)–(456), p. 159 n. 259; 175 n. 275, the last three pp. containing 'The Table'.

There should be an engraving to both *Venus and*

Adonis and *Tarquin and Lucrece*, but the plates being the same as that executed for Rowe's 1714 edition, the impressions are consequently inferior.

This second edition of Pope's may be considered as complete in 8, 9, or 10 volumes, though no set is known with it printed 'I   ne Volumes' if it corresponds with the G.T.

THEOBALD'S FIRST EDITION

NEXT in succession, Lewis Theobald, worthily titled 'The Porson of Shakespearian criticism', launched his edition in 1733 in 7 vols., 8vo, as follows:

G.T. Vol. I. 'The | Works | of | Shakespeare: | in | Seven Volumes. | = | Collated with the Oldest Copies, and Corrected; | with Notes, Explanatory, and Critical: | By Mr. Theobald. | = | I, Decus, i, nostrum: melioribus utere Fatis. Virg. | = | London: | Printed for A. Bettesworth and C. Hitch, | J. Tonson, F. Clay, W. Feales, | and R. Wellington. | = | MDCCXXXIII.

There is a dated contents title to vol. i, the other volumes have a similar title preceded by a half-title and are not contained in the alphabet or pagination. This also applies to the general title and fine portrait by G. Duchange in vol. i, but there are no engraved plates to the plays as Lowndes erroneously stated; he has only recently been corrected.

Collation. 8vo. Vol. I. ‡², A, a–e, B–Z, Aa–Ii⁴. pn. 14 pp. n.n.+ (i)–lxviii+18 pp. n.n.+(1)–(488), of which the 7 of p. 137, and 3 of p. 348 are misplaced.

Vol. II. ‡², B–Z, Aa–Mm⁴. pn. 4 pp. n.n.+(1)–536.

Vol. III. ‡², B–Z, Aa–Mm. pn. 4 pp. n.n.+(1)–(544), last leaf being a blank, the 1 of 61 not printed.

Vol. IV. ‡², A–Z, Aa–Ii. pn. 4 pp. n.n.+(1)–(512). p. 189, the 9 having slipped. The last page has 'Addendum'.

Vol. V. ‡², A–Z, Aa–Gg⁴. pn. 4 pp. n.n.+(1)–472. p. 56 the 6 imperfect.

Vol. VI. ‡², B–Z, Aa–Gg. pn. 4 pp. n.n.+(1)–464. p. 213 the 1 elided, 236 n. 336.

Vol. VII. ‡², A–Z, Aa–Ii⁴. pn. 4 pp. n.n.+(1)–494+10 pp. of 'A Table' n.n. p. 205 n. 520.

The preliminary leaves to vol. i: the two titles, 4 pp.; a dedication to the Earl of Orrery, 10 pp.; the preface, 58 pp., of which pp. iv to xv contain 'Some particulars of his private Life', based on Rowe's edition but with some fresh matter. This is succeeded by criticisms of Pope and his edition, besides acknowledgements of help from Dr. Thirlby, The Rev. W. Warburton, Martin Folkes, Esq., Dr. Mead, Dr. Friend, F. Plump-tree, and Thomas Coxeter, Esqrs. Theobald states that he has consulted over 800 old English plays. Following this are 5 pages of poems by Milton, Davenant, and Jonson, concluding with 13 pages of subscribers' names, amongst which Pope's name does not appear.

At Trinity College Library, Cambridge, is Capell's copy of this edition, formerly belonging to Warburton, with the following note by Capell on the verso A5, vol. i:

'This copy of Mr. Theobalds edition was once Mr. Warburtons who has claim'd in it the Notes he gave to the former, which that former deprived him of and made his own and some Passages in the Preface, the Passages being put between hooks and the Notes signed with his name. E.C.'

The sequential order of the plays is again altered and the doubtful ones omitted. A 'Table of the several Editions of Shakespeare's Plays, collected by the Editor' (corrected in erratum to 'Collated') contains one play of which no copy is now known. 'The excellent History of the Merchant of Venice. With the extream Cruelty of Shylock the Jew; and the obtaining of Portia by the Choice of three Caskets. As it hath been sundry times publikely acted by the King's Majesties Servants at the Globe. Written by W. Shakespeare. Newly corrected, augmented, and amended. London: printed by R. Young for John Smethwicke, and are to be sold at his Shop in St. Dunstans Churchyard in Fleet-street, under the Dyall, 1637. 4to.' This is also repeated in the 1740 edition. There are grave doubts as to whether

it ever existed, yet on the other hand his description of
Romeo and Juliet, 1637, by the same printer and publisher, accords with those we have, and it bears the
mark of veracity in the oddness of its reading. On the
other hand an edition was published in 1637 for L.
Hayes, who seemed to have held the rights until then.
Possibly he may have parted with them that year.

Seventy-five of this carefully printed edition were
done on royal 8vo, l.p., $9\frac{1}{2}'' \times 5\frac{1}{2}''$.

THEOBALD'S FIRST EDITION (DUBLIN)

THE first Irish edition of Theobald's was published in
Dublin in 1739, 7 volumes, 12mo. Although no set
had hitherto been recorded, it has been generally recog-
nized, from the existence of two or three odd volumes
and a few plays published the same year, which appeared to be reissues or excerpts, that such an edition
was no chimera. Nearly simultaneously with a notifica-
tion that the Folger Library possessed a set, one was
acquired by the writer in the original binding and
nearly superb condition, making it possible to furnish
a collation and description. Considering that the copies
subscribed for amount to only some 134, the number
of sets published may have been less than 200; and the
purchasers appearing to be of those who buy for use
rather than ornament, it is not surprising that this is
undoubtedly the rarest of any edition published in this
period. From a cursory examination, the preface, text,
and notes follow those of the first English edition, and
are therefore not to be confounded with the second
edition, London, 1740, in which the notes were abbre-
viated, though valuable for its embellishment of the
Gravelot plates.

Apart from the size, the only apparent differences
from the first edition are as follows. The omission of
the portrait, and the names of the subscribers, but the
latter is balanced by the subscribers' names to the Dublin

edition appended to vol. vii. In the same volume, to the table of the editions 'Collected' is corrected to 'Collated', but the 'Frailty' erratum is omitted and not corrected in the text of *The Merry Wives*, it was in the 1740 edition. In glancing through the list of subscribers, one notes they are mostly everyday Hibernian folk, only about three of them being titled, whereas some seventy of that class subscribed to the first edition. This set is now in the possession of the Shakespeare Library of the City of Birmingham, and so far as is known the only complete one in any public library in the British Isles.

The First Irish Edition of Theobald's, 7 vols., 12mo, 1739

General Title. Vol. I. 'The | Works | of | Shakespeare: | in | seven volumes. | = | Collated with the Oldest Copies, and Corrected; | With Notes Explanatory, and Critical. | By Mr. Theobald. | = | I. Decus, i, nostrum: melioribus utere Fatis. Virg. | = | Dublin: | Printed for John Smith at the Philosophers- | Heads on the Blind-Key; and Abraham | Bradley at the Two Bibles opposite to Syca- | more-Alley in Dames-street, Booksellers. | = | MDCCXXXIX.'

To this and to each of the other volumes is a volume title, on which the contents are enumerated and each accords with those of the first edition. The titles read: 'The | Works of | Shakespeare: | volume the . . . . | containing | [contents] | = | Dublin: | [imprint] | MDCCXXXIX. |', and excepting that to vol. i all are rubricated. The imprints are similar to the general title and where there is a variation a note of such will be found in the volume collations. Preceding the contents titles to vols. ii to vii is a half-title, undated, and printed in black, 'The | Works | of | Shakespeare. |' between rules. Though the titles are contained in the alphabet, they are not embraced in the pagination, except in vol. iii.

Collation. Vol. I. 12mo. a–c, B–X. pn. 12 pp. n.n.+(i)–liv+6 pp. n.n.+(1)–(480), of which 118 n. on inside margin; 138 n. 338; 280 n. 80; 383 n. 483; 435 n. 335. The last page is occupied with 'Books Printed' for John Smith and Abraham Bradley, and note may be made that in this collation the general and contents titles are allocated as being a6 and a7 imposed in front of a1. b6 is printed B5 and H$_2$ thus H$_z$.

Vol. II. The V.T. is similar to that of vol. i except that 'Works' 'Shakespeare' 'containing' 'Dublin' and the date are in red. The imprint is the same.

Collation. ‡², B–Z. pn. 4 pp. n.n.+(1)–532, in which there is an elision of pp. 361 to 364; 278 n.n. and 519 n. 531. The headline p. 525 'What what you will'.

Vol. III. V.T. as vol. ii, but with a stop to 'Shakespeare' instead of a colon, and imprint thus: 'Printed for John Smith, at the Philosophers Heads on | the Blind-Key; and Abraham Bradley, | at the Two Bibles in Dame's-Street: | = | M,DCC,XXXIX.

Collation. A–Z⁶. pn. (1)–(540); the last 2 pp. contain advertisements of books printed for Smith and for Bradley. Z5, misprinted Z3. The headlines pp. 132, 154 'Witner's'.

Vol. IV. V.T. as vol. ii.

Collation. ‡², A–X⁶, Yᴵ. pn. 4 pp. n.n.+(1)–(494), the last 2 pp. containing the 'Addendum', of which 20 n.n.; 140 n. 340; 354 n. 358; 364 n. 346; 368 n. 320; 372 n. 243; 373 n. 325; 376 n. 328; 377 n. 329; 380 n. 332; 381 n. 333; 431 n. 433.

Vol. V. V.T. as vol. iii, but with a stop to 'Street'.

Collation. A–U⁴. pn. 4 pp. n.n.+(1)–(460), the last 2 being blanks; 114 n. 411; 132 n. 32; 394 n. inner margin. The headline to p. 283, 'Tiomn'.

Vol. VI. V.T. The imprint as vol. ii, except that the spacing of 'Philoso- | phers' and 'Sy- | camore' are so.

Collation. ‡², A–T. pn. 4 pp. n.n.+(1)–456, of which 63 n. inner margin; 239 n. 293; and 446 n. 436.

Vol. VII. V.T. The imprint as vol. vi.

Collation. A–Y⁸, (oo⁴). pn. 4 pp. n.n.+(1)–494+10 pp. of table and 8 pp. of 'Subscribers Names | For Mr. Theobald's | Shakespeare', of which pp. 3, 6, 7, and 126 and the last 18 n.n.

The blank pages at the end of the plays and the play-titles, with dramatis personae on verso, are generally

THE

WORKS

OF

SHAKESPEARE:

IN

SEVEN VOLUMES.

Collated with the Oldeſt Copies, and Correᴄ̌ted;
With NOTES Explanatory, and Critical.

By Mr. *THEOBALD.*

I, Decus, i, noſtrum: melioribus utere Fatis. Virg.

DUBLIN:

Printed for JOHN SMITH at the *Philoſophers-
Heads* on the *Blind-Key*; and ABRAHAM
BRADLEY at the *Two Bibles* oppoſite to *Syca-
more-Alley* in *Dames-ſtreet*, Bookſellers.

M DCC XXXIX.

The General Title to the firſt Dublin edition of Theobald's,
of which only two complete ſets are known to exist.

not numbered, and where the sequential numeration is correct these have not been mentioned. The play titles coincide with those of the first edition, are printed in black between rules and without imprint, and of them *The Two Gentlemen, The Merry Wives, Much Ado, Henry VI, Parts I, II, and III, Julius Caesar*, and *Coriolanus* have catchwords; the others are without.

THEOBALD'S SECOND EDITION, 1740

THE last edition to be considered is the second of Theobald's, as follows:

Vol. I. The | Works | of | Shakespeare: | in | Eight volumes. | Collated with the Oldest Copies, and Corrected: | With Notes, Explanatory, and Critical: | By Mr. Theobald. | = | The Second Edition. | = | I, Decus, [&c.]. Virg. | = | London: | Printed for H. Lintott, C. Hitch, J. and R. Tonson, | C. Corbet, R. and B. Wellington, J. Brindley, | and E. New. | = | MDCCXL.

8 vols. 12mo. The contents title follows the general title, but in the remaining 7 volumes the contents are printed on the volume title, which is also printed partly in red. There is a portrait by G. Van der Gucht, and the whole of the plays are illustrated with the charming plates drawn by Gravelot, about half of them being also engraved by him and the others by Van der Gucht. None of these are included in the alphabet or pagination.

Vol. I. 12mo. A, a, B–R. pn. 48 pp. n.n.+(1)–(384), the last 2 pp. being blank; p. 214 n. 14.
Vol. II. A–S. pn. (1)–(432), the last 2 pp. being blank.
Vol. III. A–S⁶. pn. (1)–(420).
Vol. IV. A–U⁶. pn. (1)–(468), the last 2 pp. being blank.
Vol. V. A–R. pn. (1)–(408)   ,,   ,,
Vol. VI. A–U⁶. pn. (1)–(468)   ,,   ,,
Vol. VII. A–S⁶. pn. (1)–(420).
Vol. VIII. A–S⁶. pn. (1)–342+12 pp. table and 66 pp. index n.n.
It would be an exceptional state for a set to have all these blanks.

Many of Theobald's notes of the first edition are
omitted, but the addition of the frontispieces compen-
sates. The table at the end of vol. vii contains the
several editions collated by him, but the preface is cur-
tailed about 14 pp., with his reasons for so doing.

TONSON'S AND WALKER'S COLLECTIONS
(*All printed in 12mo.*)

IN 1734 and 1735 two collections of the whole of the
plays were published, but neither can be regarded as an
edition, though generally recorded as such when bound
up in 8 or 7 volumes. The plays composing them were
primarily published as separate plays, and volume titles
were afterwards issued for the convenience of those
who had bought or subscribed for the whole. In these
collections, particularly the one printed for Tonson,
which is the more common, seeing that two or more
issues of some of the plays were made in the same year,
uniformity is not to be expected; in fact sometimes
some of Walker's are bound in cheek by jowl with
those under Tonson's volume title, and in some volumes
one finds plays as early as 1732 and as late as 1736.
After Tonson had published several of the plays it was
decided to issue volume titles for the whole of them, and
they must have been printed nearly simultaneously, as
all of them have the curious imprint MDCXXXV (for 1735).

The title to Vol. I: The | Works | of Shakespeare. |
In eight volumes. | Volume the First. | containing, The
Tempest. | The Two Gentlemen of Verona. | The
Merry Wives of Windsor. | Measure for Measure. |
The Comedy of Errors. | Much Ado about Nothing. |
≡ | London: Printed for J. Tonson, and the rest of the |
Proprietors. | = | MDCXXXV.

The titles of the other 7 volumes read as in vol. i, but
'In eight volumes' is omitted; 'Love's Labour Lost' is
so printed in the title of vol. ii. The contents differ
but follow the sequential order of Rowe's 1714 edition.

With the play of *Thomas Lord Cromwell*, 'Some Account of the Life, &c.' (Rowe's) was published together with a portrait frontispiece from the worn Du Guernier plate. It covers 22 pages, A2–A12, and on the verso of the last leaf is the dramatis personae to the *Cromwell* play; in this state it is often bound in vol. i in juxtaposition to the *Tempest*. To remedy this, it was later reprinted on 20 pages with 'Dramatis' as catchword on the last page, so that it might be inserted to precede any play.

This collection has sometimes been erroneously dubbed as Pope's. This is untrue, and it would be difficult to assign it definitely to either of the preceding editions. To quote a few examples:

The Tempest, 1735, p. 4: 'Exeunt' and 'Re-enter Boatswain' is similar to Theobald's. Pope's version is 'Exit' and 'Re-enter', Rowe's 'Exit' and 'Enter'. A few lines below the stage direction, which was not rectified till later, reads 'A plague upon this howling—a cry within Re-enter Sebastian'. Theobald's is similar. Pope's reads 'Enter Sebastian', and Rowe followed the bad textual reading of the folio. The *Merry Wives*, 1734, perpetuates the original error in Rowe's 1714, in which the last scene of Act III is numbered scene iii instead of v. Pope divided this Act into seventeen scenes.

On the other hand the *London Prodigal* has a peculiar fault in pagination, jumping from p. 24 to p. 97, and corresponds then in pagination 97 to 130 with the 1728 edition of Pope's, though the type was entirely reset.

Many more curious deviations from the then accepted texts might be cited, but such are rather outside the scope of the present article.

Another complete collection was published by Walker, with titles as follows:

Vol. I. The| Dramatick Works| of| William Shakespear.| Volume I.| Containing the Six following Plays, viz.| I. Hamlet, Prince of Denmark, a Tragedy.| II.

Julius Caesar, a Tragedy. | III. The Life and Death of King Richard III. | with the Landing of the Earl of Richmond, and | the Battle of Bosworth-Field being the Last between | The Houses of Lancaster and York. | IV. The Life and Death of Thomas Lord | Cromwell. | V. The Tempest, A Comedy. | VI. The Merry Wives of Windsor, A Comedy. | = [of small ornaments]| London: | Printed by R. Walker, Printer of Shakespear's, | and all other English Plays, at Shakespear's | Head in Turn-again Lane, Snowhill. | = | MDCCXXXIV.

The volume has a crude frontispiece after the style of Rowe's 1714, printed partly in red, and preceding *Hamlet* is an abbreviation of Rowe's 'Life', 'Some Account (&c.)', 28 pp.

The succeeding volumes have each a volume title in red and black enumerating the plays. The same imprint is used except for variation in dates and spacing.

The contents of the volumes are as follows:

Vol. II. Macbeth, Othello, Henry IV, 1st Part, Titus Andronicus, Measure for Measure, The London Prodigal. MDCCXXXIV.

Vol. III. Antony and Cleopatra, Pericles, King Lear, Henry IV, 2nd Part, The Puritan, Two Gentlemen of Verona. MDCCXXXIV.

Vol. IV. Sir John Oldcastle, Locrine, Henry V, Timon, Comedy of Errors, A Midsummer Night's Dream. MDCCXXXV.

Vol. V. Henry VI, 1st Part, Henry VI, 2nd Part, Henry VI, 3rd Part, Henry VIII, As You like It, Merchant of Venice. MDCCXXXV.

Vol. VI. King John, Troilus and Cressida, Richard II, Romeo and Juliet, Taming of the Shrew, Love's Labour's Lost. MDCCXXXV.

Vol. VII. A Winter's Tale, Coriolanus, Cymbeline, A Yorkshire Tragedy, Twelfth-Night, Much Ado, All's Well. MDCCXXV.

THE
Dramatick WORKS
OF
William Shakefpear.
VOLUME III.

Containing the Six following PLAYS, *viz.*

I. ANTONY and CLEOPATRA, a Tragedy.

II. PERICLES, Prince of TYRE, a Tragedy.

III. The Hiftory of King LEAR, and his Three Daughters.

IV. The Second Part of HENRY IV. with the Humours of Sir JOHN FALSTAFF.

V. The PURITAN: Or, The Widow of WATLING STREET, a Comedy.

VI. The Two GENTLEMEN of VERONA, a Comedy.

LONDON:

Printed by R. WALKER, Printer of *Shakefpear's,* and all the other ENGLISH PLAYS, at *Shakefpear's* Head in *Turn-again-Lane, Snowhill.*

MDCCXXXIV.

A Volume Title to the R. Walker printed plays. Complete sets of this collection are scarce.

Note may be made that Walker issued the titles as and when the plays were being printed, whereas Tonson's were presumably printed all at once and some of them even before the plays were printed. A description and collation of these plays with their variants will follow amongst the separate plays.

THE POEMS

INASMUCH as the Poems accompanied most of the editions of the sets a short description of them will be advisable.

In 1707 vol. iv, 'Poems | on | Affairs of State', was published, and contains 'The Rape of Lucrece. Written by Mr. | William Shakespeare, and dedicated | to the Right Honourable the Earl of Southampton', pp. 143–204. It contains the argument, and has marginals indicating the most trenchant points. This is followed, pp. 205–44, by 'Venus and Adonis, | Written by Mr. Shakespear | ', the two comprising leaves K8 to R2 (misprinted S2). They are well printed, and on the whole contain no more errors than the 1710 edition of Curll's. It is notable that the previous printings appear to have been *Lucrece* in 1655 and *Venus* in 1675; and it is to these two that Rowe refers to in the 'Life', 1709, p. xxxix: 'He writ likewise, Venus and Adonis, and Tarquin and Lucrece, in Stanzas, which have been printed in a late Collection of Poems.'

The Poems, sm. 8vo, by Lintott, followed directly after Rowe's edition was published, and in part went through two printings, described farther on. Curll in 1710 issued a supplementary volume for Rowe's, 1709, designated vol. vii. It was printed in 8vo to accord with the ordinary edition, and some few were also printed on large and better paper. A collation of this and the three other editions will be found accompanying that of the sets.

The 1710 edition was reprinted in 12mo, in 1714, to form a vol. ix of Rowe's edition, 1714, but without

'The References to Classic Authors' and 'The Table'. In 1725 a volume, large 4to, was published to accompany Pope's first edition; and in 1728 the 1714 edition was reprinted in 12mo with a preface and dedication by Dr. Sewell, and the table was reintroduced to form a vol. x for Pope's second edition of that date.

Here follows the description of Lintott's editions.

The Poems, printed for B. Lintott (*c.* 1709), are extant in three states, and some of these differ also in imprint.

They were firstly published in one volume as follows:

A | Collection | of | Poems, | viz. | I. Venus and Adonis. | II. The Rape of Lucrece. | III. The Passionate Pilgrim: | IV. Sonnets to Sundry Notes of Mu- | sick. | = | By Mr. William Shakespeare. | = | [O. small fleur-de-lis arranged in triangular form] | = | London, | Printed for Bernard Lintott, at the Cross- | Keys between the Two Temple Gates in | Fleetstreet. || [*c.* 1709].

Sm. 8vo. A², B–K, L⁴–M². pn. 4 pp. n.n.+(1)–(156).
(*BH. Quaritch*)

The separate titles are respectively dated 1630, 1632, 1599, and 1599. The catchword on A2 verso is generally '*To*' but in some copies it is '*Ve*'. A variant of the title had printed at the bottom 'Price bound One Shilling Six-pence'. (*Boston, BH.*)

Shortly afterwards this volume was issued with the addition of a second volume, and an extra title was added as follows:

A | Collection | of | Poems. | In Two volumes; | Being all the Miscellanies of Mr. William | Shakespear, which were Publish'd by | himself in the Year 1609, and now cor- | rectly Printed from those editions. | The First Volume contains, I. Venus and | Adonis. II. The Rape of Lucrece. | III. The Passionate Pilgrim. IV. Some | Sonnets set to sundry Notes of Musick. | The Second Volume contains One Hundred and | Fifty

Four Sonnets, all of them in Praise of | his Mistress.
II. A Lover's Complaint of | his Angry Mistress. | = |
London: | Printed for Bernard Lintott, at the Cross-
Keys | between the Two Temple-Gates in Fleet- |
street || [*c.* 1709].

8vo. †1, A², B–K, L⁴–M². pp. 6 pp. n.n.+(1)–(156), last page a
blank. Advertisement on A2 and catchword on verso 'VE'.

Vol. II as follows: A | Collection | of | Poems, | In
Two Volumes; | Being all the Miscellanies of Mr.
William | Shakespeare, which were Publish'd by | him-
self in the Year 1609, and now cor- | rectly Printed from
those Editions. | The Second Volume, which contains, |
I. One Hundred and Fifty Four Sonnets, all | of them
in Praise of his Mistress. | II. A Lover's Complaint of
his Angry Mi- | stress. | = | London: | Printed for
Bernard Lintott, at the Cross-Keys | between the Two
Temple-Gates in Fleet-Street. ||

8vo. A², B–H². pn. 4 pp. n.n.+(1)–(100); last leaf a blank or
with an advertisement on verso, then sometimes inserted preceding
title. (*B.M. copy* H2 *a blank.*)   (*Adler, Quaritch*)

A variant of this first edition has this imprint to the
first title, 'London: | Printed for B. L. and Sold by O.
Lloyd, near | the Church, in the Temple'. || and to the
second volume, 'London: Printed for B. L. and Sold by
O. Lloyd, near | near [*sic*] the Church, in the Temple'. ||
                                                    (*P. & C.*)
In this variant, on the verso of (†) the general title,
is an advertisement of 'Books lately Publish'd'; the verso
of the last leaf of vol. ii contains a similar notice.

The two volumes were again published, vol. i being
reprinted, and some copies have only the general title
to that volume and all the subtitles have imprint 'Printed
in the year 1609'; vol. ii is identical with the previously
described.

The collation to Vol. I would then read: A², B–K,
L⁴–M²; 4 pp. n.n.+(1)–156. The imprint is generally,
'Printed for Bernard Lintott', but variations may be
extant.

In the second edition of Jane Shore by N. Rowe, 1714, the last leaf has 'Books Printed for Bernard Lintott', with the following advertisement: 'A Collection of Poems in two volumes: Being all | the Miscellanies of Mr William Shakespear which were | publish'd by himself in the Year 1609. And now cor- | rectly printed from those Editions, on an Elzyver Letter. | Price 3s.'

A copy of this was supposed to be in the Boston Public Library, U.S.A., but such is not the case: it is probable that an issue was made by Lintott at this date, possibly undated, but so far research has failed to unearth one.

Seemingly unrecorded, and therefore claiming mention here, is an article in the form of a letter of over 8 pages by Lewis Theobald on 'Shakespeare' in vol. ii of 'Miscellaneous | Observations | upon | Authors, | Ancient and Modern. | London: | Printed for Tho. Wotton, [&c.] M.DCC.XXXI.–II', narrow 4to (edited by T. Jortin). The matter dealt with is chiefly in regard to 'Corrections of a few passages in which they (Shakespeare's Poems) have suffered injury from the Printer'. They are of much interest and many seem feasible, though probably these emendations have been duly considered by the authorities on the text.

THE TONSON-WALKER QUARREL

PRIOR to dealing with the separate plays, the Copyright Act of 1709, which came into force April 1710, might be considered. By this Act, in regard to all books already printed, the authors in their own right, booksellers, printers, or other persons who had acquired the printing rights, were confirmed in the sole right of printing for twenty-one years and no longer; and the author of any book thereafter to be printed, for a period of fourteen years, and at the expiration, if the author should be then living, with a renewal for a like term.

Therefore any rights that Tonson or others had in the Shakespeare Folios, or Quartos, or Rowe's edition, would lapse in 1731. From this date or thereabouts, there is a remarkable increase in the editions, and one of the attempts of Tonson and his confrères to try to establish or continue a perpetual copyright comes within the purview.

Much expense and litigation (two Parliamentary Bills passed the Commons in 1735 and 1737, but were shelved in the Lords), and nearly every means short of actual murder were attempted by Tonson and the so-called proprietors to gain their ends for over forty years, but they were finally beaten in the Lords in 1774, who confirmed the original Act of 1709.

During 1734–5 the output of Shakespeare's plays reached high-water mark, and from what may be gathered from the extraneous matter published with the plays both by Tonson and Walker, the feud betwixt these two throws much interesting and valuable light on the practices even then in vogue to quell competition in business circles. Mainly on the evidence of the actual printed matter which reveals much acrimony (vide *The Times Literary Supplement*, 30 Nov. and 28 Dec. 1922, in which most of the advertisements have been published), one may surmise the position to have been somewhat as follows:

J. Tonson, established firmly as the premier bookseller and publisher, in combination with the other chief members in the trade, having successfully launched the first two editions of both Rowe and Pope, early in 1734 determined to print and issue at short intervals the whole of the plays separately with a frontispiece. Designating themselves as 'The Proprietors', they imagined, and possibly at first innocently (giving them the benefit of the doubt), that they were endowed in perpetuity, as had been previously the custom, to what copyright assets remained in the succession of the Folios and possibly the Quartos, and they therefore resented any infringement of their rights. These plays were intended to be sold in the theatres, or by hawkers, as well as in their several shops, to a public awakened to and appreciative of the transcendent literary merit of these dramatic works in which the wit of the ages is compacted in some thirty-six, or including the debatable, forty-three plays.

On the other hand, a certain Robert Walker, established as a printer in Turn-again Lane, Snow-Hill, who had probably been executing work for Tonson and printing the plays in particular, in 1734 commenced to sell these plays direct to the public under his own imprint; he may in the first instance have aimed at getting rid of surplus stock beyond the requirements of the trade, without fully considering the risk of losing a large portion of his customers' business. An examination of the type and ornaments used discloses that early in the year he was printing for Tonson and the others, but the fact remains that, having started on this policy and being uninclined to be subservient or dictated to, despite the dangers of legal proceedings, loss of his printing trade, and deliberate threats to ruin him, he went forward with his project. Eventually, through a very strenuous and harassing period, he published the whole of the plays and issued general title-pages to every six or more plays so that they might be bound up in convenient volumes, a proceeding similar to that adopted by Tonson. The seven general titles are dated 1734 and 1735.

Tonson, besides the notices which he printed with the plays, requisitioned the assistance of W. Chetwood, then prompter at the Drury-Lane Theatre, who declared that Walker had no help from him in the supply of copies as used at the theatres, and moreover designated his editions as piratical. Chetwood's notice was printed in many of the plays. It appears that originally the price of these plays was 1s. per copy. Walker started selling *The Merry Wives of Windsor* at 4d., thereupon Tonson reduced his price to 3*d*., and eventually down to 1*d*. per play of three sheets.

The result of this duel does not seem to be recorded. J. Tonson died in 1735 (Walker refers to him being ill of the stone), and Walker does not appear to have published Shakespeare's plays under his own imprint later than that date, but he continued doing so with the imprint 'In the Year'. In 1736 it appears that W. Feales, after Tonson's death, purchased Walker's interest in the plays, including the stock; these were disposed of with the fresh titles 'Printed in the Year 1735, or 1736' (here classed as *Walker's* in the collations). By the way, a curious omission occurs in Plomer's *Dictionary of Booksellers and Printers 1668–1775*: the notice of Jacob Tonson III, who succeeded his father in 1735, seems to be omitted.

To revert to R. Walker, an injunction was granted against him in 1739, for an edition of *Paradise Lost*, which he obeyed, but J. Osborn, who was in like case, refused, and fought the monopolists. Walker was again proceeded against in 1752, but dared Tonson to have it tried in Common Law; Tonson refused, and so the matter fell through. Walker is heard of at Cambridge, printing in partnership with T. James, but he still retained his retail shops in London, and is believed to have died between 1758 and 1764.

Developing a retail business from his printing shop, he made remarkable strides in the short space of twelve months or thereabouts, opening three establishments mainly for the sale of the plays. The number of variant imprints (there are at least fourteen) used by him during this period ranks amongst some of the remarkable records in the annals of publishing, and is an interesting example of the gentle art of advertising. A predecessor of his whose reputation lies chiefly on his piracies and unauthorized editions, H. Hills, issued at least twenty imprints during 1708–10, varying chiefly in the spacing, but Walker's mostly differ in matter and order.

As Tonson's advertisements appear in many of the plays, it may be as well to give some of them *in extenso*.

'Advertisement. | J. Tonson, and the other Pro-prietors of the | Copies of Shakespear's Plays, designing | to finish their Edition now publishing, | with all speed, give notice, That with the | last Play they will deliver Gratis general | Titles to each volume of the whole Work, | so that each Play may be bound in its pro-| per Place: and also do give further Notice, | That any Play of Shakespear's that now is, | or hereafter shall be out of Print, will be re-|printed without Delay; so that all Gentle-|men who have bought these Plays shall not | be disappointed, but may depend on hav-|ing their Sets compleated. | N.B. Whereas one R. Walker has proposed | to pirate all Shakespear's Plays, but thro' | Ignorance of what Plays are Shakespear's, | did in several Advertisements propose to print | Oedipus King of Thebes, as one of | Shakespear's Plays; and has since printed | Tate's King Lear instead of Shakes-|pear's, and in that and Hamlet has omit-|ted almost one half of the genuine Editions | printed by J. Tonson and Proprietors: The | World will therefore judge how likely they are | to have a compleat Collection of Shakespear's | Plays from the said R. Walker.'

This advertisement appears in *Oedipus*, London, printed for J. Tonson (&c.), 1734, though it did not appear in that of 1733; differently spaced, it is found added to some of the Shakespeare plays and indicated by 'T.W.'

The other of frequent occurrence reads:

'Advertisement. | Whereas, R. Walker, with his Ac-complices | have printed and publish'd several of | Shakespear's Plays; and to screen their Innu-|merable Errors, advertise, That they are | Printed as they are Acted, and industrious-|ly report that the said Plays are printed | from Copies made use of at the Theatres; I | therefore declare in Justice to the Proprie-|tors, whose Right is basely invaded, as well | as in Defence of myself, That no Person | ever had, directly or in-directly from me, any | such Copy or Copies; neither wou'd I be ac-|cessary on any Account in imposing on the | Publick such Useless, Pirated, and Maim'd | Editions, as are publish'd by the said | R. Walker. | W. Chetwood, Prompter to His | Majesty's Company of Comedians at | the Theatre-Royal in Drury-Lane.'

Sometimes this occupies a whole page, and in others half a page only, indicated respectively by 'C.L.' and 'C.S.' There are naturally variations in spacing, but the wording is similar in Tonson's and Chetwood's notices.

THE LIFE

'Some | Account of the Life, Etc. | of | Mr William Shakespear. | Written by Mr. Rowe.'

Seeing that the 'Life' was issued at least in three states to supplement the plays printed in 1734–5, a short résumé of the vicissitudes of its career may be appropriate.

The original version by Rowe of 1709 was reprinted in its entirety for the 1714, 12mo, edition. Pope, for his edition of 1725, altered it with elisions and additions, and this was reprinted for his second edition of 1728.

Tonson in 1734 issued the latter as an adjunct to the play of *Thomas Lord Cromwell*, with the dramatis personae for that play printed on the verso of the last leaf. It was entitled as in the preceding heading, with a head-piece 'a flower in oval flanked by cornucopiae of fruit', and collates a2 to a12, 22 unnumbered pages. Afterwards, so as to make it more saleable separately, or as an addition to any other play, it was entirely reset and not so well printed with a common repeating printer's ornament as headpiece and 'Dramatis' as catchword on the last page. The collation of this is A2 to A10, 18 unnumbered pages. Tonson at the same time printed the dramatis personae to *Cromwell* on another leaf of which the recto is a blank, so as to vend the play without the 'Life'.

R. Walker, also in 1734, issued the 'Life' entitled 'Some | Account | of the | Life and Writings | of | Mr W. Shakespear.' | with a headpiece 'head in oval flanked with lamps', collating 'a', two leaves+b¹², with pagination (i)–xxviii. Probably in order to evade the Copyright Act, the version of Rowe's 1714 edition was used. It was originally printed to accompany the edition of *Hamlet*, and bears that catchword on the last page. It was comparatively easy to adapt this 'Life' for any other play by pasting a slip over the catchword, and examples are found thus.

A frontispiece portrait generally accompanies both Tonson's and Walker's issues. Tonson's is in a wretched state from the fact that the plate engraved by Du Guernier in 1714 had to do senile service. Walker did not improve the appearance by issuing a similar portrait partly printed in red. They were often requisitioned for the first volumes of their collections.

To conclude the 'Life', Theobald incorporated a large portion of Rowe's edition with some interesting fresh matter, and this forms about the first fifteen pages of his preface. It is probable that he intended to make the 'Life' a separate item as his predecessors had done, for the portrait engraved in its first state has 'p 1 : in the Life' at its base, but very few were issued so, the plate being altered and the words nearly erased for most of the issue.

This 'Life' of Theobald's does not appear to have been excerpted and printed separately up to 1740, but it was reprinted in Theobald's first Irish edition, 1739, and in the second edition, London, 1740.

AN ACCOUNT OF THOMAS JOHNSON

In Great Britain, except in a few scarce instances, there were no plays of any author published separately in small 8vo or 12mo form until after Rowe's 1714 edition, whereas T. Johnson, bookseller at The Hague, by

1712 had published at least forty, nine of them being either Shakespeare's or based on his plays. Many of them found their way here, and the passing of the 4to and the advent of the 12mo may be largely attributed to the enterprise of this Dutch publisher. The possibilities of this lucrative development were not grasped by the Londoners, or at least they made little move in that direction till about 1720. The plays published at The Hague were printed on exceptionally good paper, in good clear type, and not inferior to the best productions of the London printers; taking into account that the bulk of them were printed in Holland, it is remarkable how few spelling mistakes occur therein. Complete sets of the first issue of these plays are amongst the scarcest items of this period. Considering that T. Johnson was the undoubted pioneer of these small editions, and that his first efforts were given to Shakespeare, it may be apropos to record what is known of him. This I am enabled to do through the courtesy of M. Nijhoff, of The Hague, and to a particular friend of his, Dr. E. F. Kossmann, the premier authority on the history of bookselling there.

Thomas Johnson, an important publisher at The Hague, was born about 1677 (and was possibly of Scotch extraction). He had to wife Jane Weems, and lived at The Hague from 1701 until 1728, whence he moved to Rotterdam (*vide* 'The Lawyer's Fortune' by Viscount Grimston with imprint 'Rotterdam: | Printed and Sold by T. Johnson, 1728', in which he advertises Burnet's 'History', Buckingham's Works, and Shakespear's Plays), where he continued his bookselling business till the time of his death in 1735. Before he commenced publishing books in English in any quantity, his chief output had been in Latin and French, but when he left The Hague he disposed of these and retained his stock of English works. Probably the Copyright Act contributed to the development of this branch of his business. He was a member of 'the

Association of Booksellers at The Hague', and many of
his publications bear the imprint 'Printed for the Company of Booksellers'. At his death his widow, conjointly
with his son Alexander, carried on the business, but
removed again to The Hague in 1741, where it continued until 1745. The remaining stock was purchased
by Hendrik Scheurleer in 1750-1, who published under
his own name a whole series of these plays in sixteen
volumes containing about sixty-four plays, many of
them bearing the imprints of the 1711–20 editions,
possibly being actual remainders of the 1720 issue. To
revert to T. Johnson. About 1720 he was a member of
the Society of The Hague and London Booksellers, and
must have worked in accord with some of the latter,
seeing that, apart from the plays, 'The | Works | of Mr.
Alexander Pope.' | [with imprint] 'London. | Printed by
T.J. for B.L. & other Booksellers. | = | M.DCC.XVIII',
small 8vo, was vendible here: B.L. is assumed to be
Bernard Lintott. The three minor titles in this book
bear imprint 'London. | Printed for T Johnson. | = |
MDCCXVI'; the items are separate entities; and on the last
leaf is a catalogue of forty-five plays priced at 6*d*. and 8*d*.,
of which eight are Shakespearian. In 'Phaedra | and |
Hippolitus. | A | Tragedy | = | By Mr. Edmund Smith. |
= | [O. monogrammic T.J.] | Printed for T Johnson. |
In the Year 1711', small 8vo, A–F⁴, one finds printed
on the last 6 pages, 'A Choice Collection of all the best
English | Plays neatly and correctly printed in small |
Volumes fit for the pocket, | & sold by T. Johnson
Bookseller at the Hague'; and at the end of the first list,
'These 40 Plays make 10 handsom Volumes, | when
bound together: They are also sold single, at | the
prices here mark'd', the first eight being Shakespeare's
or adaptations by Dryden, Davenant, and Granville.
Following this list are four pages of plays, 'Other Plays
now printing, or proposed to be | printed, to make this
Collection complete'. This second list comprises ninety-
six plays, and the first four are *Timon* (by Shadwell),

King Lear (Tate's), *Troilus and Cressida* (Dryden's), *K. Henry IV, 2nd Part.* Only the first and last of these are recorded. Two others are mentioned: *Anthony and Cleopatra*, by Sir Charles Sedley, and *Caius Marius*, by Otway, which are not traceable, if printed.

Further evidence of his activities on this side appear in the works of John Sheffield, 1723, vol. ii. In order to replace the castrated pages 69–102, the elision of the two essays is supplied in some copies by 'Buckingham restor'd', 'printed by T. Johnson in the year 1727'; and in Burnet's 'History', 'London, Printed for the Company of Booksellers', 1725, v. iii, are two lists of books sold by Johnson, plays (53 titles) and English books (9 titles).

It is generally accepted that 'London', as an imprint to all his publications, is spurious, research having failed to trace any possibility of any having been printed in the British Isles. Moreover, the tail-pieces used are similar to those used by the Amsterdam printers. Possibly the most conclusive evidence is that in nearly all the books published by him the alphabets extend beyond the moiety of the leaves: a common practice abroad, but of very exceptional occurrence here. I am indebted to the researches of F. O'Kelley, Esq., of The Bibliographical Society of Ireland, for light on this printers' custom. As to whether Johnson was actually the printer, there are no records available. Seeing that the Dutch publishers, without having their own printing office, nevertheless stated in their advertisements that they printed their publications, and Johnson used the 'London' imprint with intent to deceive, we may fairly disregard 'Printed by J.T.' He probably employed the same printer for most of his work, as the ornament used for the title of *Othello*, 1710, was used for his publication, *Histoire de l'Empire Ottoman*, 1709, and the head-piece to *Hamlet, Macbeth*, and *Julius Caesar*, 1710–11, was used to Joncourt's *Quatre Lettres sur les Jeux de Hazard*, 1713, and the tail-piece to *Hamlet* finds a place there as well.

Whilst this work was in the press the following information has been kindly supplied by M. Nijhoff.

The imprint and contents of vol. i of the set in the Royal Library at The Hague, 16 vols. (849 A. 2), are: 'Printed for the Company of Booksellers' (no dedication); and the plays are *Julius Caesar*, 'London, Printed for the Company of Booksellers', 80 pp., *Macbeth*, 'London, Printed for the Company', 76 pp., *Hamlet*, 'London, Printed for T. Johnson', 119 pp., *Othello*, 'London, Printed for the Company', 108 pp. For fuller collation *vide* the separate plays. The date of publication is *c.* 1720–1.

These do not appear to have been reprinted, but Scheurleer, having bought the whole of the remainder of Johnson's stock, issued the plays separately and in sets, with general title to the volumes 'A Select | Collection | of the | Best Modern English Plays' | 'Printed for H. Scheurleer, Junior. | at the Hague, 1750.' There were probably 16 volumes, one in the writer's possession states 'Vol. XIV'.

Of the sets in The Hague Royal Library, one in 10 volumes (846 E. 19), vol. i contains *The Ambitious Stepmother*, *The Non Juror*, *The Distrest Mother*, *The Fair Penitent*. In a set of six volumes (204 L. 5) vol. i contains *Julius Caesar*, *Macbeth*, *Timon of Athens*, *All for Love*, *The Funeral*, *State of Innocence*, *Amphitrion*; and one is in the possession of M. Nijhoff, in 10 volumes, of which vol. i contains *The Funeral*, London, Printed for T. J., 1721, and *The Drummer*, *The Distrest Mother*, *The Ambitious Stepmother*, *The Tragedy of Jane Shore*, *The Fair Penitent*, all with imprint 'London, Printed for the Company', and with the 'T.J.' device.

Mr. G. Dawson, of the Folger Shakespeare Library, has courteously supplied the following description of an exceedingly scarce state of *The Merry Wives of Windsor*, 1710.

'The first issue of which we have a copy is an irregular

one which must have been issued more or less acciden-
tally. Leaf A1 was originally a title with Johnson's
early fountain ornament (as on *Othello*, 1710), with the
name of William Page in the Dramatis Personae on the
verso. Before the printing was completed, some one
noticed that the editor had excised the only scene in
which William appears and that his name ought, therefore, to be omitted from it. Also it was decided that
the title-page ought to mention 'The Amours of Sir
John Falstaff'. Therefore a new title was set up
including this, and one line was removed from the type
of the Dramatis Personae and printed on leaf F6, which
would otherwise have been blank. Most copies have
the new title with 'The Amours' and a smaller ornament—flowers, leaves, and fruit. This is a cancel,
attached to a stub. Our copy has the original title as
A1 and the second title as F6. The original title is thus:
The | Merry Wives | of | Windsor. | A | Comedy.
| Written by Mr. W. Shakespear. | [O.] | London. |
Printed in the Year 1710.'

'A COLLECTION OF THE BEST ENGLISH PLAYS'

THIS series of Dutch published plays is extant as collections in three differing states, largely dependent on
the dates they were issued. Approximately the first
came out from 1710 to 1718, and comprises forty-eight
plays in 12 volumes. Originally it was projected in 10
volumes, 1711–12, but supplemented *c.* 1714 and 1718
by two others, increasing the number of plays from
forty to forty-eight.

The second issue appeared from 1720 to 1722 in
16 volumes, and included those previously published
with sixteen additional plays.

The third was issued in 1750 by H. Scheurleer, jun.,
also in 16 volumes, and containing similar plays.

There are complete sets of the last two issues in the
Royal Library at The Hague. A complete set of the

first is not recorded in England. The British Museum set of the first 10 volumes, excepting vols. i and x, is of the second issue.

By reason of its scarcity a description is here given. The title of volume i reads as follows. 'A | Collection | of the best | English Plays. | vol. i. | Containing, | Julius Caesar; | Macbeth; | Hamlet; | Othello: | (bracketed) By Mr. Wm. | Shakespear. | [O. T.J. intertwined in image and reflection] | Printed for T. Johnson, | Bookseller at the Hague. | = | M.DCC.XI.'

This is followed by four pages of dedication, of which this is the first portion. 'To Her | Royal Highnes | the | Princess of Wales; | &c. &c. &c. | Madam, | Allow me, on the happy & long wished | for occasion, of Your Royal Highness | passing this way to England, to lay at your | feet this Collection of the best Dramatick Pieces | of our most eminent English Poets. Many of | these Plays have been countenanced & favou-|red by our Soverains themselves, & by others | of the Royal Family; & I hope the whole | Collection will not be thought unworthy of | Your Royal Highnes's acceptance nor | unfit for the diversion of some of your leisure | hours. The Stage when duly regulated, affords | not only the most refined diversion to polite | persons, but also the most lively & usefull | Instructions: & I doubt not Your Royal | Highnes will find the English Stage may | deserve your countenance & protection, which | will soon raise it to a degree of perfection far | beyond any other that has been in the | World. This will give great satisfaction to | all the polite part of the Nation, & parti-|cularly to the fair Sex, which there, in | many respects, outshines all the World. (&c).'

Now the Princess of Wales as such did not exist till 27 September 1714, when her husband's patent was sealed. She stayed at The Hague from the 17 to 20 October on her journey to England, and was possibly presented with a set of these plays then, therefore this dedication could not have been printed many days prior

A
COLLECTION

OF THE BEST

ENGLISH PLAYS.

V O L. I.

Containing,

JULIUS CÆSAR; ⎫
MACBETH; ⎪ By *Mr. Wm.*
HAMLET; ⎬ *Shakespear.*
OTHELLO: ⎭

Printed for T. JOHNSON,
Bookseller at the Hague.

M. DCC. XI.

The General Title to volume i of the first
edition of The Hague published plays, issued
originally in ten but extended to twelve volumes.
Only one set of the first issue recorded.

(Folger)

to that date. These two dedication leaves are not contained in the alphabet. The complete set did not appear
in 1711; the bulk of it was published in 1712. There
are many possible explanations of this, and it would be
of interest if a copy of vol. i should turn up with a
presumably earlier dedication. Possibly there was no
dedication originally, as Queen Anne was fonder of the
apron than the sock and buskin.

Without further digression the collation runs:

Sm. 8vo. ‡¹, *², A–F⁵, A–F², A–H, A–H², the alphabet extending
to 5 in each case. pn. 6 n.n.+(1)–90, (1)–(84), (1)–(128), (1)–114.
There is a stub to the title (‡) which suggests the possibility of an
earlier dedication.

The title-pages correspond with those described in
the separate plays (q.v.), and in all other particulars.

Vol. II. Title. 'A | Collection | of the best | English
Plays. | Vol. II. | Containing IV. Plays | Of Mr. Will.
Shakespear. | K. Henry IV. & S. I. Falstaf. | The
merry Wives of Windsor. | The Tempest, or Enchanted
Island. | The Jew of Venice. | [O. T.J. intertwined] |
Printed for T. Johnson, | Bookseller at the Hague. | = |
M.DCC.XII.'

Sm. 8vo. ‡¹, A–G², A–F⁵, A–G, A–E². pn. 2 pp. n.n.+(1)–100,
(1)–90, (1)–112, (1)–(68).

The plays correspond with the separate issues.

Of the remaining 10 volumes, 8 were published in
1712 with general titles as vol. i and imprint 'Printed
for T. Johnson | = | Anno M.DCC.XII.', the contents
being described on each of them. They are as follows.

Vol. III. Dryden's Aurenge Zebe, All for Love,
Oedipus, and Spanish Fryar.
Vol. IV. Dryden's Indian Emperor, State of Inno-
cence, Don Sebastian, and Amphitrion.
Vol. VI. Etherege's She wou'd if She cou'd, Man of
Mode, Buckingham's Rehearsal, and Chances.
Vol. VII. Congreve's Old Batchelor, Double Dealer,
Love for Love, and Way of the World.

Vol. VIII. Congreve's Mourning Bride, Smith's Phaedra, Tuke's Adventures, and Wycherley's Plain Dealer.

Vol. IX. Cibber's Love's Last Shift, Careless Husband, and Vanbrugh's Provok'd Wife, and Aesop.

Vol. X. Steel's Funeral, Farquhar's Constant Couple, Recruiting Officer, and Beaux Stratagem.

Vols. XI and XII are probably dated 1714 and 1718.

Vol. XI should contain Addison's Cato, Rowe's Jane Shore, Philip's Distrest Mother, and Timon of Athens, 1712 (Shadwell's).

Vol. XII should contain Jonson's Volpone, Rowe's Ambitious Step Mother, Tamerlane, and Jane Shore.

The play titles will have imprints similar to the general titles or 'Printed for T. Johnson. | In the Year', or 'London, | Printed in the Year', or with 'London' omitted, but all should be dated—and some of them earlier than the volume title. All have printers' ornaments or devices; the monogrammic T.J. intertwined is the more common, and there are three differing blocks of it: The Fountain (vide *Othello*), Flower Basket (vide *Tempest*), Fruit Spray (vide *Merry Wives*), and a Flower Spray are all used.

In the second issue the volume titles generally read: 'A | Collection | of the best | English Plays, | Chosen out of all the best | Authors. | Vol. . . . | [O. T.J. device.] | London. Printed for the Company of Booksellers.' (N.D.). It consisted of 16 volumes containing the forty-eight of the first issue, though the first eight of Shakespearian interest were reset entirely, with the addition of sixteen further plays ranging in dates from 1718. These volumes were probably published from 1720 to 1722, and the play titles, where they are not remainders of the first issue, bear the imprints: 'London, | Printed for the Company'. (N.D.), 'London, Printed for T. Johnson | = |' (date), 'Printed for T.J. & are sold by the Book-|sellers of London and Westminster. | = |' (date),

'Printed for T. J. In the Year' (date), or as the volume title. For the fresh plays the T.J. device was generally used.

As no contents are on the volume titles, the sequential order varies, and as it is computed that the whole of Johnson's output amounted to not less than seventy plays, some may appear in one set and not in another.

The third state appeared in 1750 in 16 volumes with general titles thus: 'A Select | Collection | of the | Best Modern English Plays | ≡ | Selected from | the | Best Author's. | = | Vol. . . . | = | [O. common] | Printed for | H. Scheurleer, Junior. | at the Hague, 1750.' The imprint on the separate plays appears to be chiefly 'London. | Printed for the Company'. Many of the plays were reprinted, but it is possible that the Shakespeare plays that were reprinted in 1720–1 were again published in these volumes, where the imprint is similar. The lists of *English Plays* still appear at the end of some of the plays '*sold by T. Johnson*', though the business had passed into other hands.

UNRECORDED PLAYS

OF a certainty this list of the separate plays cannot be complete: unrecorded imprints or variants are sure to turn up from time to time. Some that are recorded only very briefly are not available for verification, and some may have escaped attention. For such omissions and errors the reader's pardon is craved, and may the measure of the iniquity be balanced with further gleanings to garnish the stores of Shakespeare lore. Tracing the text of these plays to their sources may prove an interesting task, but any short notes attached to the plays regarding this are without authority.

There are many editions that do not appear to be now extant, and to some of the series of plays a note of those which have not been located, but culled from contemporary publishers' advertisements, will be appended. Research may unearth some of these later, and if they can be retrieved, one of the objects of this collation may be attained.

Apart from The Hague 'Collection of English Plays', there were the following published: *The English Theatre*, London: Printed for W. Chetwood at Cato's Head in Russell Street, Covent Garden. (N.D.) in 6 or more volumes containing separate plays with dates 1714 to 1722. There is *The English Theatre*, 1731–3, also 12mo in 26 volumes, and *The Beauties of the English Stage*, 1739, in several volumes; this is not to be confounded with a similarly titled 2 volumes containing many Shakespeare quotations printed for Ward and Chandler, 1737. All these contain separately printed editions.

Of these plays some are exceedingly scarce, only one or two copies being known. As a rough guide, all the Dublin printed and The Hague published, the anonymous Walker 'Printed in the Year —', most of those by Feales and Darby, and the few Quartos, may be reckoned in that category; so also may the adaptations by Betterton, Bullock, Burnaby, Carrington and Bellamy, Cibber, Dennis, Hughes, Johnson, Lacey, and Theobald. With a few exceptions the plays printed in 1734–5 by Walker are very much scarcer than those by Tonson.

With regard to the editions, apart from the large paper of Rowe's, the second edition is much the scarcer of the two printed in 1709, and the 12mo edition of 1714 is by no means common in a good state. The second edition of Pope (Grierson and Ewing, Dublin, 1726), is very scarce: even odd volumes seldom turn up. But the edition of Theobald (Dublin, 1739), comes well within the rare class, only two or three sets being known; in fact till very lately its existence as a complete set had not been recorded. G. Risk, Dublin, advertised in 1726 as follows: 'Shakespear's Works, 8 vols. 1l. 8.s. ... For and Sold by G. Risk, G. Ewing, and W. Smith. Booksellers in Dame's Street.' No set or odd volumes have been traced with this imprint, though it is possible it may have referred to that published by Grierson and Ewing; some on the other hand may have been issued to include Risk and Smith, who were both booksellers of consequence.

In 1724 a now scarce little book in two volumes appeared which deserves recording. It is entitled as follows: 'Thesaurus Dramaticus. | Containing all the Celebrated | Passages, Soliloquies, | Similes, Descriptions, | and other Poetical Beauties | in the | Body of English Plays, | Antient and Modern, | Digested under Proper Topics; | with the | Names of the Plays, and their Authors, | referr'd to in the Margin. | ≡ | In Two Volumes. | ≡ | Vol. 1. | ≡ | Purissima Mella Stipant. Virg. Georg. | ≡ | London: | Printed by Sam. Aris, for Thomas Butler, | next Bernard's-Inn in Holborn. MDCCXXIV.'

> 12mo. ‡1, A⁶, B–L. pn. F. 2 pp., Title 2 pp. (i)–x+(1)–240. Vol. ii, a similar title with motto 'Utile Dulci'. ‡² B–P, Q¹¹. pn. F. 2 pp., Title 2 pp. (1)–358. The frontispieces are by the Van der Guchts, and respectively depict Apollo and Tragedy and Mercury and Comedy. (*B.H.*)

In the List of Plays (some 174) and Authors, twenty-nine are Shakespeare's with the addition of eleven adaptations or alterations; nearly one-fourth of the whole—a goodly company. It is probable that this is the first comprehensive list of the alterations published.

THE ABBREVIATIONS

To avoid repetition the two imprints of Tonson and the thirteen of Walker have been tabulated along with the supplementary abbreviations applicable to the separate plays.

> All words or dates underlined thus are printed in red.
> SHO. = Shakespeare's head in oval.
> FO. = P. Fourdrinier.
> LDG. = Lud. Du Guernier.

TW. = Tonson's advertisement in regard to general titles and warning against Walker's editions.

CS. = Chetwood's small notice.

CL. = Chetwood's full-page notice.

The dates after the frontispieces indicate their previous appearances.

In most instances the location of the plays examined is given with abbreviations somewhat as follows: (*Adler*) N. C. Adler, Esq., London; (*B.H.*) Birmingham Shakespeare Memorial Library; (*B.M.*) The British Museum; (*Bod.*) Bodleian Library; (*Boston*) The Boston Public Library; (*Dobell*) Dobell Bros., London; (*F. O'Kelly*) F. O'Kelly, Esq., Dublin; (*Folger*) The Folger Shakespeare Library, Washington; (*H.N.P.*) H. N. Paul, Esq., Philadelphia; (*J. de L.S.*) J. de Lacey Smythe, Esq., Dublin; (*McLeish*) McLeish Bros., London; (*Mich.*) The Michigan College Library, U.S.A.; (*N.L.D.*) National Library, Dublin; (*P.&C.*) Pickering & Chatto, Ltd., London; (*Phil. Univ.*) Philadelphia University; (*Quaritch*) Bernard Quaritch, Ltd., London; (*Rosenbach*) Dr. Rosenbach, Philadelphia; (*S.*) H. L. Ford; (*S.B.L.*) Shakespeare Birthplace Library; (*T.C. Camb.*) Trinity College, Cambridge; (*T.Col. Dublin*) Trinity College, Dublin; (*V.A.M.*) Victoria and Albert Museum; (*Yale*) Yale University Library.

TONSON'S IMPRINTS

(A) = 'Printed for J. Tonson, and the rest of the | Proprietors; and sold by the Booksellers | of London and Westminster. | = '

(B) = 'Printed for J. Tonson, and the rest of the Pro-|prietors; and sold by the Booksellers of | London and Westminster. | ='

WALKER'S IMPRINTS

(1) Printed by R. Walker, in Turn-again Lane, near | Fleet-Lane, by the Ditch-side. | = |
    (*Hamlet; M.W. of Windsor*, without hyphen to 'Fleet'.)

(2) Printed by R. Walker, at Shakespear's Head in | Turn-again-Lane, Snowhill. | = | (*J. Caesar*)

(3) Printed by R. Walker at Shakespear's Head in Turn-|again Lane, Snow-hill. | = | [date] | [Price 4*d.* with the Frontispiece.]
    (*Rich. III; M. for M.; M. W. of W.* without 'Price'.)

(4) Printed by R. Walker, at Shakespear's-Head, in | Turn-again Lane, by the Ditch-side. | = |
    (*Cromwell; London Prodigal; Othello; Tempest; Macbeth; Henry IV, Pt. 1; J. Caesar.*) With [Price 4*d.* with the Frontispiece.] (*Richard III.*) With no rule preceding date (*Titus And.*).

(5) Printed by R. Walker, at Shakespear's-Head, in | Turn-again Lane, by the Ditch-side; and may be | had at his Shop the sign of Shake-

spear's Head in | 'Change-Alley, Cornhill, and likewise at his Shop, | the Sign of Shakespear's Head, between the Savoy | and Somerset-House, in the Strand. | = | (*Verona; Pericles; Hamlet*)

(6) Printed by R. Walker, at Shakespear's Head, | next the White Horse-Inn in Fleet-Street. | = | (*Coriolanus*)

(7) Printed by R. Walker, at Shakespear's-Head, in | Turn-again Lane, by the Ditch-side; and may be | had at his shop the sign of Shakespear's Head in | Change-Alley, Cornhill. | = | (*Henry VIII*)

(8) Printed by R. Walker, at Shakespear's-Head, in | Turn-again Lane, by the Ditch-side; and may be | had at his Shop the Sign of Shakespear's Head in | Change-Alley, Cornhill, and likewise at his Shop, | the Sign of Shakespear's Head and Hawk, between | the Savoy and Somerset-House, in the Strand. | = |
    (*Oldcastle; Antony & C.; Locrine*)
Hyphen after 'again', comma after first 'Shop', and all the 'Heads' hyphenated.   (*King Lear*)

(9) Printed by R. Walker at Shakespear's Head in Turn | again Lane, by the Ditch-side; and may be had at hī | Shop, the sign of Shakespear's Head in Change-Alley | Cornhill; and likewise at his Shop, the sign of Shake-|spears Head and Hawk, between the Savoy and Somer-|set-House, in the Strand. | = | (*Puritan*)

(10) Printed by R. Walker, at Shakespear's-Head, in | Turn-again-Lane, by the Ditch-side; and may be had | at his Shop, the Sign of Shakespear's-Head, in Change- | Alley, Cornhill. | = |
    (*Taming of the S.; Troilus; Romeo and J.; K. John; M. of Venice; Henry V; As You Like It; Mid. N. D.*). 'Heads' without hyphens and no comma to second 'Head' to *Timon* and *Henry IV, Pt. 2.*

(11) Printed by R. Walker at Shakespear's Head in Turn-|again Lane, by the Ditch-side; and may be had at his | Shop, the Sign of Shakespear's Head, in Change-Alley, | Cornhill. | = |
    (*Rich. III; Love's L. L.; Much Ado; 1st, 2nd, 3rd Henry VI; C. of Errors.*) Hyphen after 'Alley' instead of comma. (*Cym.; Twel. N.; Wint. Tale*)

(12) Printed by R. Walker, next the White | Horse-Inn in Fleet Streeet. [*sic*] | = | (*All's Well; Yorkshire Tr.*)

(13) Printed by *R. Walker*, Printer of Shakespear's, | and all the other English Plays, at Shakespear's | Head in Turn-again-Lane, Snow-hill. | = | [The imprint to the volume titles but with a variation in spacing to vol. v, with the dates in red.]

DESCRIPTION AND COLLATION OF
THE SEPARATE PLAYS

ALL'S WELL

1. All's Well | that | Ends Well. | A | Comedy. | = | By Mr. William Shakespear. | = | [O. basket of fruit] | ≡ | London: | (B) | MDCCXXXIV.

> 12mo. A–C, D⁶. pn. (1)–(84). FO. plate extra (1728, 1714). (T.W.) advertisement on last p.
> The first separate edition. (*B.M., S.*)

2. All's Well, | that | Ends Well; | A | Comedy. | = | By Shakespear. | = | [O. woman's head in floriated oval] | = | London: | [W. 12] M.DCC.XXXV.

> 12mo. A–C, D⁶. pn. (1)–(84). FO. plate in reverse extra. Last p. blank. (*B.H., B.M., S.*)

3. All's Well, | that | Ends Well: | A | Comedy. | = | By Shakespeare. | = | [O. Britannia holding out shield] | = | London: | Printed in the Year M.DCC.XXXV.

> 12mo. A–C, D⁶. pn. (1)–(84). FO. plate engraved in reverse extra. Last p. blank.
> A reissue of Walker's with dramatis personae reset only. (*S.*)

ANTONY AND CLEOPATRA

4. All for Love, or, The World well Lost. | = | [1701].

> Folio. From H3–P1. pn. 53–106.
> Being an excerpt from vol. ii, The | (Comedies), | Tragedies, | and | Operas | Written by | John Dryden, Esq; | = | Now first Collected together, and | Corrected from the Originals. | = | In Two Volumes. | = | London, | Printed for Jacob Tonson, at Gray's-Inn-Gate in Gray's-Inn-Lane; | Thomas Bennet, at the Half-Moon; and Richard Wellington, at | the Lute in St. Paul's Church-Yard. MDCCI.
> The overline of date is a black line. (*S.*)

5. Beauty | The | Conquerour: | Or, the Death of | Marc Antony. | A | Tragedy. | In imitation of the |

Roman way of Writing. | = | Written by Sir Charles
Sedley, Baronet. | = | Never before Printed. | = |
London: | Printed, and Sold by John Nutt, near
Statio-|ners-Hall. 1702.

> 8vo. Aa–Dd. pn. (1)–64. Bb3 and Cc3 respectively printed B3
> and C3.
> An excerpt from *The Works of Sir Charles Sedley, Bart.*, of the
> same date. (*B.H. P.&C.*)

6. All for Love: | or, The | World well Lost. | A |
Tragedy, | Acted by Her | Majesties Servants. | = |
Written in Imitation of Shakespear's Stile, | By Mr.
Dryden. | = | Facile est verbum [&c.] Cicero. | = |
London, | Printed for J. Tonson, and T. Bennet. Sold
by R. Wellington, | G. Strahan, and B. Lintot. 1703.

> 4to. a, A–I. pn. 16 pp. n.n.+1–(64). (*Adler, B.H.*)

7. All for Love: | Or The | World well Lost. | A |
Tragedy, | Acted by Her Majesty's Servants. | = |
Written in Imitation of Shakespear's Stile, | By Mr.
Dryden. | = | Facile est verbum [&c.] Cicero. | = |
London, | Printed for J. Tonson: And Sold by J.
Knapton at the Crown in | St. Paul's Church-yard,
G. Strahan over-against the Royal-|Exchange in Corn-
hill, and E. Sanger at the Post-House at the | Middle-
Temple Gate. 1709.

> 4to. A, a, B–I. pn. 16 pp. n.n.+1–(64). (*Adler, B.H.*)

8. All for Love: | or, the | World well lost. | A |
Tragedy. | Written in Imitation of Sakespear's [sic]
Stile, | By Mr. Dryden. | = | Facile est verbum [&c. 2
lines]. | [O. fountain with horse and ass, with motto
'Non sibi sed omnibus'] | London, | Printed in the
Year 1710.

> 8vo. A–F, G⁶. pn. (1)–(108).
> This is one of the series of plays published by T. Johnson at The
> Hague, and is also found in vol. iii of *A Collection of the Best
> English Plays, 1712.* A scarce edition. (*Folger*)

9. All for Love: | or, The | World well Lost. | A | Tragedy. | As it is acted at the | Theater-Royal, | By | His | Majesty's Servants; | And Written in Imitation of Shakespear's Style. | = | Facile est verbum [&c. 3 lines]. Cicero. | = | Printed in the Year MDCCXVII.

12mo. From H2 to M4. pn. 25 pp. n.n., being (171–195)+196–(272).

An excerpt from Dryden's *Dramatick Works* of 1717. In the dramatis personae Booth plays Marc Antony and Mrs. Oldfield Cleopatra. (*S.*)

10. All for Love: | or, The | World well Lost. | A | Tragedy. | As it is Acted at the | Theater-Royal, | By | His Majesty's Servants; | And Written in Imitation of Shakespear's St [sic] | = | Facile est verbum [&c. 3 lines]. Cicero. | = | Printed in the Year MDCCXVII.

12mo. From H2 to M4. pn. 25 pp. n.n., being (171–195)+196–(272).

An excerpt from Dryden's *Dramatick Works* of 1718. Mr. Hart plays Marc Antony, and Mrs. Boutell Cleopatra. The type was entirely reset. (*S.*)

Dryden's *Dramatick Works* were published in 6 volumes with imprint to vol. i: 'Printed for Jacob Tonson at Shakespear's Head | over-against Katharine-Street in the Strand. | MDCCXVII.'

Shortly after, the Duke of Newcastle gave an order, at his own expense, for the erection of a monument to Dryden in Westminster Abbey, whereupon the edition of the previous year was issued with a new title-page with imprint thus: 'Printed for J. Tonson; And Sold by J. Bro-|therton and W. Meadows, at the Black | Bull in Cornhill. MDCCXVIII.' Immediately following the contents title was added a dedication 'To His Grace the | Duke of Newcastle, |' consisting of 24 pp. n.n. by William Congreve in which is a delightful appreciation of Dryden as a friend and a master poet. The bulk of the plays are a reissue of the 1717 edition, but *All for Love* was entirely reset, the stock of the first printing having possibly run out or for the reason of it being then newly acted with a different cast.

11. All for Love: | or, the | World well Lost. | A | Tragedy. | Written in Imitation of Sakespears [sic] Stile, | By Mr. Dryden. | = | Facile est verbum [&c.]

Cicero. | = | [O. T.J. monogrammic device] | Printed for T. Johnson. M.DCC.XX.

Sm. 8vo. A–F, G⁴. pn. (1)–(104). Last leaf blank.
A variant of this imprint is 'Printed for the Company of Book-sellers'. (*B.M.*)

12. All for Love: | or, The | World well Lost. | A | Tragedy. | As it is acted at the | Theatre Royal, | By His Majesty's Servants; | and Written in Imitation of Shakespear's Style. | = | Facile est verbum [&c.] Cicero. | = | London: | Printed for J. T. and Sold by T. Jauncy, at the | Angel without Temple-Bar. MDCCXX.

12mo. A–D, E⁶. pn. (1)–(108). The first 2 pp. and last p. blank.
p. (107) contains the 'Epilogue'. (*S.*)

13. Antony | and | Cleopatra: | A | Tragedy. | As it was Acted at the Duke's | Theatre. | = | By the Honourable Sir Charles | Sedley, Bart. | = | London: Printed in the Year 1617 [sic].

12mo. K3 to K6, L–P in sixes. Q2. pn. (103)–174.
An excerpt from 'The | Works | of the Honourable Sir Charles Sedley, Bart. | in Prose and Verse. | London: Printed for S. Briscoe, at the Bell Savage-|Inn on Ludgate-Hill, and Sold by T. Bickerton, | in Pater-Noster-Row, 1722. (*B.M.*)

14. Caesar | in | Aegypt. | A | Tragedy. | As it is Acted at the | Theatre-Royal in Drury Lane, | = | Written by Mr. Cibber. | = | Aufer ab aspectu [&c.] Lucan. Lib. 9. | = | London: Printed for John Watts at the Printing Office | in Wild-Court near Lincolns-Inn-Fields. | = | MDCCXXV. | [Price 1s. 6d.]

8vo. A², B–F. pn. 4 pp. n.n.+1–(80). (*B.H.*)

15. All for Love: | or, The | World well Lost. | A | Tragedy. | As it is Acted at the | Theater-Royal, | By | His Majesty's Servants; | And written in Imitation of Shakespear's style | = | Facile est verbum [&c. 3 lines]. Cicero. | = | Printed in the Year MDCCXXV.

12mo. From H2 to L, M⁴. pn. 25 pp. n.n. being (171)–(195)+ 196–(272).
The play Hp., fountain and cupids. Tp., mask and banner.
An excerpt from vol. iv of Dryden's 1725 edition (vide *Tempest*).
(*Dyce, V.A.M.*)

16. All for Love: | or, The | World Well Lost. | A | Tragedy. | As it is Acted at the Theater-Royal, | by His Majesty's Servants; | and written in Imitation of Shakespear's Style. | = | Facile est verbum [&c.] Cicero. | = | London: | Printed for J. Tonson in the Strand. | = | MDCCXXVII.

12mo. A–D, E⁶. pn. xxx pp. n.n.+(1)–(78). (*P.&C., B.H.*)

17. All for Love: | or The | World well Lost. | A | Tragedy. | As it is Acted at the | Theater-Royal, | by His Majesty's Servants; | And Written in Imitation of Shakespear's Style. | = | Facile est verbum [&c.] Cicero. | = | London: | Printed for J. Tonson in the Strand. | = | MDCCXXVIII.

12mo. A–D, E⁶. pn. xxx n.n.+(1)–(78) including a half-title.
(*P.&C., S.*)

18. All for Love: | or, | The World well lost. | A | Tragedy. | = | Written in Imitation of Shakespear's Stile, | By Mr. Dryden. | = | Facile est verbum [&c.] Cicero. | = | [O. vase of flowers supported by birds] | = | Dublin: | Printed by and for Geo. Grierson, at the | Two Bibles in Essex-Street. MDCCXXX.

12mo. A¹², B–G, in sixes. pn. (1)–96. B3 printed B5. (*Ed., B.H.*)

19. All for Love: | or, the | World Well Lost. | A | Tragedy. | Written in Imitation of Shakespear's Stile, | By Mr. Dryden. | = | Facile est verbum [&c.] Cicero | = | [O.] | = | Dublin: | Printed by S. Powell, | For Thomas Moore, Bookseller, at | the Corner of Dirty-Lane in Dame's-|street. MDCCXXXI.

12mo. A–C, D⁴. pn. (1)–(80). The last leaf contains a list of Philip Crampton's publications. (*Ed., Uni. Lib.*)

20. Antony | and | Cleopatra. | A Tragedy. | = | By Mr. William Shakespear. | = | [O. small mask with birds] | = | London: | [A] M.DCC.XXXIV.

> 12mo. A–D. pn. (1)–(96), excluding FO. plate (1728). CL. on the last page. A variant in spacing of imprint with date in line with Westminster. (*B.M., B.H., S.*)

21. Antony | and | Cleopatra. | A | Tragedy. | As it is Acted at the | Theatres. | = | By Shakespear. | = | [O. woman's head in floriated roundel] | = | London: | [W. 8] MDCCXXXIV.

> 12mo. A–D. pn. (1)–(96), including F. re-engraved after FO. p. 94 is blank, and pp. 95 and 96 have Walker's advertisement terminating 'Scraps and Nonsense'. *Vide* No. 94.
> Some copies are without this last leaf D12. (*B.M., B.H., S.*)

22. All for Love: | Or The | World well Lost. | A | Tragedy. | By Mr. Dryden. | Facile est verbum [&c.] Cicero. | [O. SHO.] | London: | Printed for J. Tonson in the Strand. | = | MDCCXXXV.

> 12mo, in twelves. From H to H6, I–M. pn. 28 pp. n.n.+(199)–(276). F. by Gravelot.
> An excerpt from Dryden's *Works* of that date, vol. iv, the n.n. pp. being (171)–(198). Mr. Hart plays Marc Antony. (*S.*)

23. All for Love: | or the | World well Lost. | A | Tragedy. | By Mr. Dryden. | = | Facile est verbum [&c.] Cicero. | = | [O. SHO.] | = | London: | Printed for J. Tonson in the Strand. | = | MDCCXXXV.

> 12mo. H to L, M6. pn. 28 pp. n.n.+(199)–(276), An excerpt from Dryden's *Works*, 1735, a reissue. F. by Gravelot. (*B.H.*)

24. Caesar | in | Egypt. | A | Tragedy. | At [sic] it is Acted at the | Theatre-Royal in Drury-Lane, | By His Majesty's Servants. | = | Written by Mr. Cibber. | = | Aufer ab aspectu [&c. 5 lines]. Lucan. lib. 9. | = | London: | Printed for J. Watts and Sold by

W. Feales at Rowe's-|Head the Corner of Essex-Street in the Strand. | = | MDCCXXXVI.

> 12mo. A–C, D⁶. pn. (1)–(84), including F. by Van der Gucht.
> (*S.B.L.*)

25. All for Love: | Or, The World Well Lost. | A | Tragedy. | By Mr. Dryden. | = | Facile est verbum [&c. 2 lines]. Cicero. | = | [O. SHO.] | ≡ | London: | Printed for J. and R. Tonson in the Strand, | = | MDCCXL.

> 12mo. A–D. pn. (1)–(96), including F.　　　　(*B.H., Mich.*)

ADVERTISED BUT NOT RECORDED

Antony and Cleopatra

R. Wellington. 4to.	. . . . .	1705 or A.
M. Wellington. 12mo. (J. Darby for)?	. .	1718 „
J. Osborn .	. . . . . .	1721 „

All for Love

M. Wellington	. . . . . .	1718 or A
S. Chapman	. . . . . .	1721 „
W. Feales .	. . . . . .	1734 „
T. Astley .	. . . . . .	1731 „
G. Risk	. . . . . .	1729 „

AS YOU LIKE IT

26. Love in a Forest. | A | Comedy. | As it is Acted at the | Theatre Royal in Drury-Lane, | By His Majesty's Servants. | = | Nostra nec erubuit Sylvas habitare Thalia. | = | By Mr. Johnson. | = | [O. basket of flowers supported by birds] | = | London: | Printed for W. Chetwood at Cato's-Head in | Russel-street, Covent-Garden; and Tho. Edlin, | at the Prince's Arms, over-against Exeter-Exchange | in the Strand. 1723. (Price 1s. 6d.) | Just Publish'd, The Compromise, or Faults on both Sides. | A Comedy.

> 8vo. A⁴, B–E, F⁴. pn. i–(viii)+1–(72) including the half-title, the last 2 leaves containing the prologue and epilogue. Dedication 'To The Worshipful Society of Free-Masons'.　　(*P.&C., Bod.*)

27. As you Like it. | A | Comedy. | = | By Mr. William Shakespear. | = | [O. inverted music trophy] | ≡ | London: | [A] | MDCCXXIV.

> 12mo. A–C. pn. (1)–72. FO. F. extra (1728, 1714).
>
> (*B.M., B.H., S.*)

28. As you Like it. | A | Comedy. | = | By Shakespear. | = | [O. medallion woman's head in floriated oval] | = | London: | [W. 10] M.DCC.XXXV.

> 12mo. A–C. pn. (1)–72. F. by Smith after FO. extra. Some copies p. 37 n.n. (*B.M., B.H., S.*)

29. The | Modern Receipt: | or. | A Cure for Love. | A | Comedy. | Altered from | Shakespeare. | With | Original Poems, Letters, &c. | = | Ex voto fictum [&c.] Hor. | = | [O. basket of flowers] | = | London: | Printed for the Author, M.DCCXXXIX.

> 8vo. A–P, Q⁶. pn. 8 pp. n.n.+(1)–(180). Last leaf with errata and contents. Four of the preliminary pp. contain list of subscribers. The second title (Poems) is dated MDCCXXXVIII. Authors, J. Carrington and D. Bellamy. (*P.&C.*)

THE COMEDY OF ERRORS

30. The | Comedy | of Errors. | = | By Mr. William Shakespear. | = | [O. basket of fruit] | ≡ | London: | [B] | MDCCXXXIV.

> 12mo. A–B, C⁶. pn. (1)–60, exclusive of FO. plate (1728, 1714). CL. on A2. (*B.M., B.H., S.*)

31. The | Comedy | of Errors. | = | By Shakespear. | = | [O. vase of fruit floriated] | = | London: | [W. 11.] MDCCXXXV.

> 12mo. A–B, C⁶. pn. (1)–(60), exclusive of plate engraved by Smith after FO.
>
> Some copies were published finishing at C4. The two leaves C5, C6 are occupied with Walker's advertisement, commencing as follows: 'Turn-again Lane, Snow-Hill, London. Jan. 24, 1734–5 | Proposals | for Printing by Subscription, A Select Collection of Tragedies, | Comedies, Operas, and | Farces, | Written by the most Celebrated Poets, viz. | Shakespeare, Ben Jonson, Wycherley [etc.].' (*B.M.*)

CORIOLANUS

32. The | Invader of His Country: | or, | The Fatal
Resentment. | A | Tragedy. | As it is Acted at the |
Theatre-Royal in Drury-Lane. | By His Majesty's
Servants. | = | By Mr. Dennis. | = | London: | Printed
for J. Pemberton in Fleet-street, and J. Watts near |
Lincolns-Inn-Fields: And Sold by J. Brotherton and
W. | Meadows in Cornhill; T. Jauncy and A. Dodd
without | Temple-Bar; W. Lewis in Covent-Garden,
and J. Graves | at St. James's. 1720. (Price 1s. 6d.)

8vo. A–F. pn. 16 pp. n.n.+(1)–(80). p. 59 n.n.
Some copies were published without the price notice. Dennis in
the advertisement (A7^v) airs his grievances against C. Cibber and
his co-managers on the scurvy treatment he says they accorded to
him. He also makes a long plaint in his dedication to the Duke
of Newcastle. Dennis is believed to be the original of the caricature
of 'The Distress'd Poet' of Hogarth's. He was certainly one of the
stormy petrels, and affords an example of the acrimony, jealousy,
and testiness displayed by those then associated with the poetic and
dramatic arts. (*B.H.*, *S.*)

33. Coriolanus, | The Invader of his Country: | or,
the | Fatal Resentment. | A | Tragedy; | As it is Acted
at the | Theatre-Royal in Drury-Lane. | By His
Majesty's Servants. | = | By Mr. Dennis. | = | The
Second Edition. | = | London, | Printed: And sold by
J. Peele, at Lock's Head in | Pater-noster Row. 1721.
[Price 1s.]

8vo. A–F. pn. 16 pp. n.n.+(1)–(80). (*Bod.*, *Mich.*)

34. Coriolanus. | A | Tragedy. | = | By Mr. William
Shakespear. | = | [O. funeral urn and flower sprays] |
≡ | London: | [B] | MDCCXXXIV.

12mo. A–D. pn. 96 pp., exclusive of LDG. plate (1728, 1714).
Last p. numbered 86 through pp. 62–71 being duplicated. pn.
(1)–71, 62–86. p. 48 n. 40. (*B.M.*, *B.H.*, *S.*)

35. Coriolanus. | A | Tragedy. | = | By Shakespear. |

= | [O. woman's head in roundel enfoliated.] | = |
London: | [W. 6] M.DCC.XXXV.

> 12mo. A–D. pn. 96 pp., exclusive of LDG. plate engraved in
> reverse. Similar mispagination to Tonson's, 1734, except the
> sequence runs pp. 68, 72, 70, 71, 69, 63–86, but type entirely
> reset. (*B.M., B.H., S.*)

36. Coriolanus. | A | Tragedy. | = | By Shakespeare. |
= | [O. Cupid's head winged over festooned ornament]
| = | London: | Printed in the Year M.DCC.XXXV.

> 12mo. A–D. pn. 96 pp., with similar plate, mispagination, and
> type to Walker's, 1735 only the title-page and dramatis personae
> on the verso differ. (*S.*)

CYMBELINE

37. Cymbeline. | A | Tragedy. | = | By Mr. William
Shakespear. | = | [O. SHO.] | ≡ | London: | [A] |
MDCCXXXIV.

> 12mo. A–D. pn. (1)–96, exclusive of LDG. plate (1728, 1714).
> CS. on last page. (*B.M., S.*)

38. Cymbeline: | A | Tragedy. | = | By Shakespear. |
= | [O. basket of flowers] | = | London: | [W. 11]
MDCCXXXV.

> 12mo. A–D. pn. (1)–96, exclusive of LDG. plate engraved in
> reverse. (*B.M., B.H., S.*)

HAMLET

39. The | Tragedy | of Hamlet | Prince of Denmark.
| = | As it is now Acted by Her Majesties | Servants. |
= | By | William Shakespeare. | = | London. | Printed
for Rich. Wellington, at the Dolphin and Crown in
Paul's Church-| Yard, and E. Rumball in Covent Garden.
1703. | = | Newly Publish'd, some Fables [&c. 6 lines].

> 4to. A², B–L, M². pn. 4 pp. n.n.+ 1–(84). p. 1 'Barnardo' so. Last
> 2 pp. 'Books Printed'. 'Plays': *Caius Marius, All for Love, Henry
> the Sixth, Julius Caesar, Othello, Richard the Second* are advertised.
> Probably the first issue. (*Adler*)

40. The | Tragedy | of Hamlet | [&c.]——1703.
(*Another issue.*) Imprint as 39 except 'Pauls' and
'Covent-Garden' so.

> 4to. A², B–L, M². pn. 4 pp. n.n.+(1)–(84). Type entirely reset.
> 'Denmark' in running headline without stop. p. 1 n.n., the text
> teems with printers' errors. (*Adler, B.H.*)

41. The Tragedy | of Hamlet | [&c.]——1703.
(*Another issue.*)

> 4to. A², B–L, M². pn. 4 pp. n.n.+1–(84). Type again reset. p. 1
> numbered. 'Bornardo' printed so. Omitting stage-direction 'Exit
> Fran'. Headline 'Denmark' not stopped, and on last p. 'SPLY.' for
> 'PLAYS' with misprints 'Provok'd mife' and 'furmish'd'. (*Adler*)

42. Hamlet, | Prince | of | Denmark. | A | Tragedy. |
Written by | Mr. William Shakespear. | [O. mono-
grammic T.J. interwoven] | London, | Printed in the
Year 1710.

> Sm. 8vo. A–H. pn. (1)–(128).
> Printed *ostensibly* in London for publication by T. Johnson at
> The Hague. Published singly, and also in *A Collection of the Best
> English Plays*, vol. i, 1711. Actually printed in Holland. (*S.*)

43. Hamlet. | An | opera. | as it is Perform'd at the |
Queen's Theatre | in the | Haymarket. | [O. basket
of flowers decorated] | London: | Printed for Jacob
Tonson, at Shakespear's Head over-against | Catherine-
Street in the Strand. 1712.

> 8vo. A⁶, B–F, G⁴, H². pn. 4 pp. n.n. (i)–viii, +1–(92). Dedi-
> cation by N. Grimaldi. (*P.&C.*)

44. Hamlet, | Prince of Denmark. | A | Tragedy. |
As it is now Acted by his | Majesty's Servants. | =
| Written by | William Shakespear. | = | London; |
Printed by J. Darby for M. Wellington | at the King's
Head, over against St. Cle-|ment's Church, in the
Strand. 1718. | (Price One Shilling.)

> 12mo, in sixes. A–I. pn. (1)–(108), inclusive of F. engraved in re-
> verse of the LDG. plate. On the last p. 'Plays Sold by M. Welling-

ton' the following are mentioned: *Mackbeth, Timon of Athens, All for Love, Anthony and Cleopatra, Tempest, Caius Marius, Hamlet.* This is the first edition of the text revised by John Hughes, referred to by Theobald in *Shakespeare Restored,* and also the first edition in 12mo. Mr. Wilkes played Hamlet.   (*B.H., S.*)

45. Hamlet, | Prince | of | Denmark. | A | Tragedy. | = | By Mr. W^m. Shakespear. | [O. T.J. intertwined.] | London, | Printed for T. Johnson. | = | MDCCXX.

    8vo. A–E, F^6, G, H^6. pn. (1)–(120). Last verso blank.
                                          (*Mich., B.H.*)

46. Hamlet, | Prince | of | Denmark. | A | Tragedy. | = | Written by | Mr. William Shakespear. | = | [O. vase of flowers] | Dublin: | Re-Printed by Geo Grierson, at the | Two Bibles, in Essex-Street, 1721.

    8vo. A–F, G^3, H^3. pn. (1)–(108), 54 n. 4, 95 n. 9. The last page is a blank.   (*T.C. Dublin.*)

47. Hamlet, | Prince of Denmark; | A | Tragedy, | As it is now Acted by his | Majesty's Servants. | = | Written by | William Shakespear. | = | London; | Printed by J. Darby, for A. Bettes-| worth in Pater-noster-Row and F. Clay | without Temple-Bar. M.DCC.XXIII. | (Price One Shilling.)

    12mo, in sixes. A–I. pn. (1)–108. First leaf a blank. No frontispiece issued with this. Books printed for M. Poulson on last page. This is the second edition of Hughes's revised text with a few additional corrections, possibly by him, though he died in 1720.
                          (*B.H., P.&C., J.de L.S.*)

48. Hamlet, | Prince | of | Denmark. | A | Tragedy. | = | Written by Mr. William Shakespear. | = | Revised by Mr. Pope. | = | [O. goblet of flowers and leaves] | = | Dublin: Printed by and for George Grierson, at | The Two Bibles in Essex-Street. 1726.

    Sm. 8vo. A^4, B–G, H^7. pn. (1)–118, including a half-title reading 'Hamlet, | Prince | of | Denmark'. On the last p. the catchword is 'Othello'.
    This is a reprint of the play issued in Grierson and Ewing's 1726

edition of Pope, with the addition of a fresh title. It is not an excerpt, as the alphabet of this play in the set runs N6 to U7.

(*T.C. Camb.*)

49. Hamlet, | Prince | of | Denmark. | A | Tragedy. | = | Written by M. Wil. Shakespear. | = | Revised by Mr. Pope. | = | [O.] | ≡ | Dublin: | Printed by S Powell, | For Thomas Moore, Bookseller, at | the Corner of Dirty-Lane in Dame-|Street, MDCCXXXI.

12mo. A⁸, B⁴, C⁸, D⁴, E⁸, F⁴, G⁸, H⁴, I⁶. pn. (1)–108. The ornament is a common scroll. (*B.H.*)

50. Hamlet. ex. The | Life | of the | Stage. | in eight volumes. | = | Spiritus intus [&c.] Virg. Aen. | = | Vol. 1 | = | containing | The Orphan. || Oedipus. | Hamlet. || Caius Marius.| = | [O. urn] | ≡ | London: | Printed for Richard Wellington, at the Dolphin | and Crown without Temple-Bar. | = | MDCCXXXIII.

12mo, in sixes. From A3 to I6. pn. (5) [sic]–(108), lacking title and dramatis personae A1 A2.

The only copy known. It is a reprint of the 1723 edition (47) with some printers' errors, very probably that advertised by Poulson in 1731. (*B.H.*)

51. Hamlet, | Prince of Denmark; | A | Tragedy, | As it is now Acted by his | Majesty's Servants. | = | Written by | William Shakespear, | = | London, | Printed: And Sold by the Booksellers of London | and Westminster. 1734.

12mo. A–D, E⁶. pn. (1)–(108). First leaf a blank. Colophon, p. 107: 'London: Printed for J. Tonson, and the rest of | the Proprietors; and Sold by the Booksellers of London | and Westminster. | ≡ | September 12, 1734. | Advertisement | To all Hawkers of Books, Pamphlets &cet.' Offering to sell *The Merry Wives* at 1*d*. and others at the same rate, this extends to p. 108. Type entirely reset. No frontispiece issued with this originally. (*S.*)

52. Hamlet, | Prince of Denmark; | A | Tragedy, | As it is now Acted by his | Majesty's Servants. | = | Written by | William Shakespear. | = | London: |

Printed for J. Tonson, and the rest of the Proprietors; | And sold by the Booksellers of London and | Westminster. 1734.

> 12mo. A–D, E⁶. pn. (1)–(108), including LDG. plate (1728, 1714), which is leaf A. CS. on (108).   (*B.M., B.H., S.*)

53. Hamlet, | Prince of Denmark. | A | Tragedy. | As it is Acted at the | Theatres. | = | By Shakespear. | = | [O. intaglio woman's head floriated] | = | London: | [W. 5] MDCCXXXIV.

> 12mo. A–D. pn. (1)–96. F. by Smith extra.
> This is a very scarce edition based on Hughes's revision of 1718 with the notice 'This Play being too long to be acted upon the Stage, such Lines as are left out in the Acting are marked | thus ' '. The dramatis personae has the cast with Wilkes as Hamlet.   (*S.*)

54. Hamlet, | Prince of Denmark; | A | Tragedy. | As it is now Acted at the | Theatres. | = | By Shakespear. | = | [O. two-handled vase on bracket] | = | London: | [W. 1] | MDCCXXXIV.

> 12mo, in sixes. a⁶, b¹², C–G, H⁴. pn. (1)–76+(i)–xxviii, exclusive of F. by J. Smith. pp. i–xxviii contain the 'Life'; this is found inserted after the title-page, though originally it was intended to front vol. i of Walker's collection and is generally found there in the complete sets. The catchword on the last page is 'Hamlet': this occurs sometimes with a blank slip obliterating it, so that it might be used separately from this play. The alphabet of the 'Life' is: 2 leaves of a+b¹².   (*S.*)

55. Hamlet, | Prince of Denmark; | A | Tragedy. | As it is now Acted at the | Theatres. | = | By Shakespear. | = | [O. two-handled vase on bracket] | = | London: | [W. 1.] MDCCXXXIV.

> 12mo, A4, C–G in sixes, H4. pn. (1)–76, exclusive of a plate by J. Smith, in which the Queen is standing.   (*S.*)

55a. *Another variant.* 12mo. A2, B2, C–G in sixes, H4. pn. (1)–76, exclusive of the plate by J. Smith.   (*B.M.*)

55b. *Another variant.* 12mo. ‡², B2, C–G in sixes, H4. pn. (1)–76, exclusive of the plate by J. Smith. C2 printed F2. With the Life prefixed ‡² + b¹². pn. (1)–xxviii.   (*B.H.*)

56. Hamlet, | Prince of Denmark; | A | Tragedy. | As it is now Acted | By His Majesty's Servants. | = | Written by William Shakespear. | = | [O. shield] | London: Printed, and Sold by the Booksellers of London | and Westminster. | = | MDCCXXXVI. |

> Sm. 8vo. A–G. pn. (1)–112. No F.
> A very rare edition, the one at Boston being the only example, and even that lacks leaf 111–12. The Hughes's text. The Boston copy finishes on p. 110 with 'the rest in silence' the perpetuated misprint of Hughes's 1718 edition, and lacks about 52 lines. In binding, leaves E4 and E6 (pp. 71–2 and 75–6) are misplaced before E3 and E5. *(Boston)*

57. Hamlet, | Prince of Denmark. | A | Tragedy. | As it is now Acted | By His Majesty's Servants. | = | Written by William Shakespear. | = | [O. Britannia] | = | London: | Printed for W. Feales, at Rowe's-Head, over-|against St. Clement's Church in the Strand. | = | M.DCC.XXXVI. |

> 12mo, in sixes. A–I. pn. (1)–(108), including F. On verso of last leaf, 'Books printed for R. Poulson'.
> This is the first play in vol. i of *The British Theatre, in Ten Volumes, Consisting of the best Tragedies and Comedies. Collected from the most Celebrated Authors*. London, W. Feales, 1736.
> *(Phil. Univ.)*

58. Hamlet, | Prince of Denmark: | A | Tragedy. | As it is now Acted | By His Majesty's Servants. | = | Written by William Shakespear. | = | [O. eagle with wings spread] | = | London; Printed for W. Feales, at Rowe's-Head over-|against St. Clement's Church in the Strand. | = | M.DCC.XXXVII.

> 12mo. A1, B–E, F1. pn. (1)–100. F. by Dandridge extra.
> *(Adler*, uncut copy.)

59. Hamlet, | Prince of Denmark; | A | Tragedy. | Written by | William Shakespear. | = | [O. basket of

flowers] | = | London: | Printed for the Booksellers
in Town and Country. | = | MDCCXXXIX.

> 12mo, in sixes. U to Ee6. pn. (253)–(360). p. 359 at foot reads,
> 'The End of the First Volume'. Dramatis personae on p. (255).
> Excerpt from vol. i of *The Beauties of the English Stage*.
>
> (*Adler, B.H.*)

ADVERTISED BUT NOT RECORDED
Hamlet.

W. Chetwood, Lintott	1719 or A.
S. Chapman	1721 „
T. Astley	1728 „
G. Risk	1729 „
J. Poulson, and the Wellingtons . .	1731 „
W. Feales	1734 „
P. Crampton, Dublin (Pope's) . . .	1731 „

JULIUS CAESAR

60. Julius | Cæsar. | A | Tragedy. | Writen [sic] by
Mr. W. Shakespear. | [O. monogrammic T.J. device] |
London, | Printed in the Year 1711.

> Sm. 8vo. A–E, F⁵. pn. (1)–90. The 2 last leaves contain four
> songs written for Buckingham's alteration of the play.
> This edition was printed for sale at The Hague for T. Johnson. It
> is sometimes found without the last 2 leaves, as in a British
> Museum copy. The alphabet in all these Hague plays extends to
> the fifth leaf. Also found in *A Collection of the Best English Plays*,
> vol. i, 1711. (*S.*)

61. The | Tragedy | of | Julius Caesar; | With the
Death of | Brutus and Cassius: | Written Originally
by Shakespear, | And since Alter'd by Sir William |
Davenant and John Dryden, | late Poets Laureat. As
it is now Acted | By His Majesty's Company of
Comedi-|ans at the Theatre-Royal. | To which is pre-
fix'd | The Life of Julius Caesar, abstracted | from
Plutarch and Suetonius. | = | London: | Printed for
J. Tonson, and Sold by W. Mears at the Lamb | with-
out Temple Bar, W. Chetwood at Cato's Head under |

Tom's Coffee-House in Russell-street, R. Franklin at
the | Sun in Fleetstreet, and G. Strahan at the Golden
Ball in | Cornhill. | MDCCXIX.

> 12mo. A–G in sixes, H³. pn. (i)–(xii), +1–(78), including F.
> by Kirkall. The rule after Suetonius is made of small fleurs-de-lis.
> (*B.H.*)

61a. *Another issue* with the following imprint: 'London, | Printed for
W. Chetwood at Cato's | Head in Russel-Court, near the Theatre-
Royal, | and R. Francklin at the Sun over-against St | Dunstan's
Church in Fleet-street. MDCCXIX. | Price One Shilling.'
The collation is the same.   (*J. de L. S.*)

62. The | Tragedy | of | Julius Caesar; | [&c.] 1719.

> Being another issue of the 1719 edition with imprint 'London,
> Printed for G. Strahan at the Golden | Ball in Cornhill; W. Mears,
> at the Lamb | without Temple-Bar; W. Chetwood, at | Cato's Head
> in Covent-Garden; and R. | Francklin at the Sun over against
> St. Dun-|stan's Church in Fleet-street. M.DCC.XIX. | Price One
> Shilling.' Contained in 'A | Collection | of Plays | By | Eminent
> Hands | in Four Volumes. Vol. 1. Containing | Tragedies. | Julius
> Caesar. Richard the Third. [&c.] | ≡ | London: | Printed for
> W. Mears at the Lamb | without Temple-Barr. MDCCXIX.'
> The same collation.   (*B.M.*)

63. Julius | Caesar; | A | Tragedy. | Written by Mr.
Shakespear. [O. T.J. intertwined] | London, | Printed
for the Comp. of Booksellers. | [N.D. *c.* 1720.]

> Sm. 8vo. A–E. pn. (1)–80.
> The second edition of The Hague published plays.
>   (*Hague, P.&C.*)

64. Julius | Caesar. | A | Tragedy. | ≡ | By Mr.
William Shakespear | ≡ | [O. G.G. monogram with
2 sphinxes and 2 cupids] | Dublin: Printed by and
for George Grierson, at the | Two Bibles in Essex-
Street. MDCCXXI.

> 8vo. ‡1. A–D, E⁴. pn. 2 pp. n.n.+(1)–72. pp. 31 and 32
> omitted.   (*Folger*)

65. The | Tragedy | of Julius Caesar, | Altered: | With
a Prologue and Chorus; | ≡ | By His Grace, | John

Duke of Buckingham. | = | [O. phoenix] | London: |
Printed by John Barber, MDCCXXII.

> Large 4to. Ee to Tt4. pn. (209)–(328). Last leaf blank. Ee2
> printed E2.
> An excerpt from *The Works of John Sheffield*, London, 1723. (*S.*)

66. The | Tragedy | of | Marcus Brutus: | = | With the
Prologue and the Two | Last Chorus's. | = | Written
by his Grace, | John Duke of Buckingham. | = | [O.
pedestal of fruit with birds] | = | London: | Printed
by John Barker. MDCCXXII.

> Large 4to. Uu to Mmm3. pn. (329)–(454). The dramatis personae
> contains most of the J. Caesar characters, and the play is largely
> based on the fourth and fifth acts. The first and second choruses
> were written by Mr. Pope.
> An excerpt from the *Works*, 1723.   (*S.*)

66a. The Tragedy of Julius Caesar, Altered, with a
Prologue and Chorus; By his Grace John Duke of
Buckingham.——
London. | Printed for the Company. [N.D. *c.* 1722]

> 8vo. A collation of this and Buckingham's *Marcus Brutus* has
> not been obtainable. T. Johnson, in The Hague, advertised both
> these at 6*d.* each in Rowe's *Tamerlane*, and Etherege's *Man of
> Mode*, published by him *c.* 1722.

67. The | Tragedy | of | Julius Caesar, | Altered: |
With a Prologue & Chorus, | By his Grace | John
Duke of Buckingham | [O. T. J. intertwined] | London,
| Printed for the Company. [N.D. 1726.]

> Sm. 8vo. H to M2. pn. (113)–(180).
> An excerpt from The | Works | of | John Sheffield, | [&c.] | vol. i.
> Containing his Poetical Works. | = |—Nec Phoebo [2 lines]. Virg.
> | [O. T. J. intertwined.] | Printed for John Barber, Alderman of
> London. | MDCCXXVI.
> Printed in Holland. Printer's device of T. Johnson.   (*B.M.*)

68. The | Tragedy | of | Marcus Brutus: | With the
Prologue & the two last | Chorus's. | Written by his
Grace | John Duke of Buckingham. | [O. T. J. inter-

twined] | London, | Printed for the Company. [N.D.
1726]

Sm. 8vo. N to R4. pn. (185)–(256).
An excerpt from Sheffield's *Works*, 1726. Vide *J. Caesar*, same
date. Prefixed to the half-title to the *Works* are 2 leaves: 'Catalogue of
English Plays and English Books Sold by T. Johnson in the Hague.'
(*B.M.*)

69. Julius | Caesar. | A | Tragedy. | = | By Mr.
William Shakespear. | = | [O. woman's bust supported
by bouquets, &c.] | = | Dublin: | Printed by and for
A. Rhames, opposite the Pied-Horse | in Capel-Street,
MDCCXXVI.

Sm. 8vo. A⁸, B⁴, C⁸, D⁴, E⁸, F⁴. pn. 2 pp. n.n. (1)–70.   (*B.H.*)

70. Julius | Caesar. | A | Tragedy. | = | By Mr.
William Shakespear. | = | Revised by Mr. Pope. | = |
[O.] | = | Dublin: Printed by and for George Grierson,
at the | Two Bibles in Essex-Street. MDCCXXVI.

8vo. A–E. pn. (1)–(80). Last leaf a blank.
The above title is from Miss Stockwell's Catalogue. There is a
copy lacking title in the Dyce Library, S. Kensington, but with the
last blank leaf. This play was advertised in vol. viii of Grierson's
1726 edition of Shakespeare.

71. Julius Caesar; | A | Tragedy, | As it is now Acted
by his Ma-|jesty's Servants. | = | Written by | William
Shakespear. | = | [O. woman's head in quatrefoil
ornament] | = | London, | Printed for J. Tonson; and
also for J. Darby, | A. Bettesworth, and F. Clay, in |
Trust for Richard, James, and Be-|thel Wellington.
M.DCC.XXIX. | Price 1s.

12mo, in sixes. A–G. pn. (1)–(84). No. F. pp. 79–82 contain
the choruses for the first four Acts and on pp. 83–4 a list of
'Books Printed' mentioning *Hamlet, King Lear,* and *Othello,* sold
by Darby, and *Troilus and Cressida* and *Othello* in 4to.
'Prince 1s.' occurs in some copies.   (*B.H., P.&C.*)

72. The Tragedy | of | Julius Caesar, | altered: | With

a Prologue and Chorus; | = | By His Grace | John Duke of Buckingham. | = | [N.D. 1729]

> 8vo. P2 to U7. pn. 211–302. p. 244 n. 44.
> An excerpt from The | Works | of | John Sheffield, | [&c.] | The Second Edition, Corrected. | London, | Printed for J. B. and sold by Aaron Ward, [&c.] | = | M.DCC.XXIX.
> To vol. ii of this edition, unmentioned in the Index, was added [Ornamental] = | The | Castrations. | O. = | (Price One Shilling and Six-pence.) a–e in fours, f², pn. (i)–xliv.
> (*B.M., S.*)

73. The | Tragedy | of | Marcus Brutus: | = | With the Prologue and the two | last Chorus's. | = | Written by His Grace | John Duke of Buckingham. | = | [N.D. 1729]

> 8vo. U8 to Cc. pn. (303)–400.
> An excerpt. Vide *Julius Caesar*, same date. (*B.M., S.*)

74. Julius Cæsar. | A | Tragedy. | As it is Acted at the | Theatre Royal | In Drury-Lane. | By His Majesty's Servants. | = | By Mr. William Shakespear. | = | [O. SHO.] | ≡ | London: | [A] | MDCCXXXIV.

> 12mo. A–C. pn. (1)–72, exclusive of LDG. plate (1728, 1714). Theobald's dramatis personae and some of Theobald's altered text. (*B.M., B.H., S.*)

75. Julius Cæsar. | A | Tragedy. | As it is Acted at the | Theatre Royal | In Drury-Lane. | By His Majesty's Servants. | = | By Mr. William Shakespear. | = | [O. basket of fruit] | ≡ | London: | [B] | MDCCXXXIV.

> 12mo. A–C. pn. (1)–72. LDG. F. extra. CS. on last p.
> The text differs and type entirely reset, rare. (*S., Boston*)

76. Julius | Cæsar, | A | Tragedy. | As it is Acted at the | Theatres. | = | By Shakespear. | = | [O. woman's head in roundel decoration] | = | London: | [W. 2] MDCCXXXIV.

> 12mo. A–C. pn. (1)–(72), including LDG. plate engraved in

reverse by J. Smith. The dramatis personae is the enlarged one as printed in Theobald's edition of the previous year, but the text, &c., follows Rowe's, as does Walker's other issue of the same date.

(*B.M., B.H., S.*)

77. Julius Caesar. | A | Tragedy. | As it is Acted at the Theatres. | = | By Shakespear. | = | [O. male bust supporting a basket of fruit] | = | London: | [W. 4] MDCCXXXIV.

12mo. A–C. pn. (1)–(72), including LDG. plate engraved by J. Smith in reverse. With Rowe's dramatis personae.

(*B.M., B.H., S.*)

78. Julius Caesar. | A | Tragedy. | By | Mr. W. Shakespeare. | Collated with the Oldest Copies, and Corrected; With Notes Explanatory, and Critical. | = | By Mr. Theobald. | = | [O. bouquet of flowers enfoliated] | = | Dublin: | Printed by M. Rhames. | For J. Smith, Bookseller, at the Philoso-|phers-Heads on the Blind-Quay. | = | M.DCC.XXXIX.

12mo. A–C, D⁶. pn. (1)–(84).
A reprint from the *Works*, Theobald, Dublin, 1739, wherein it occupies in vol. vi, F to I6, pp. (121)–(204).

79. The Tragedy | of | Julius Caesar, | altered: | With a Prologue and Chorus; | = | By His Grace | John Duke of Buckingham. | = | [1740]

8vo. P2 to P8, Q to U7. pn. (211)–302.
An excerpt from The | Works | of | John Sheffield | [&c.] | The Third Edition [&c.] | London: | Printed for T Wotton | [&c.] | MDCCXL. (*B.M.*)

80. The | Tragedy | of | Marcus Brutus. | = | With the Prologue, and the Two last Chorus's; | = | Written by his Grace | John Duke of Buckingham. | = | [1740]

8vo. U8 to Cc. pn. (303)–400.
An excerpt. Vide *J. Caesar*, same date. (*B.M.*)

ADVERTISED BUT NOT RECORDED

Julius Caesar.

R. Wellington, 4to.	.	1705 or A.
S. Chapman, 12mo	.	1721 ,,
G. Risk, Dublin .	.	1729; also G. Ewing and W. Smith.
J. Poulson and the Welling-		
tons . .	.	1731 or A.
W. Feales . .	.	1734 ,,
J. Smith, Dublin. Shef-		
field's *Works* in 12mo		
for *Marcus Brutus* and		
Julius Caesar .	.	1739 ,,

HENRY IV, PART I

81. K. Henry IV. | With the | Humours | of | Sir John Falstaff. | A | Tragi-Comedy. | As it is Acted at the | Theatre in Litttle-Lincolns-Inn-Fields | By | His Majesty's Servants. | = | Revived, with Alterations. | = | Written Originally by Mr. Shakespear. | = | London, | Printed for R. W. and Sold by John Deeve at Bernards-Inn-Gate | in Holborn, 1700. | = | Newly Published [&c. 5 lines]

> 4to. A1, B–G, H³. pn. (1)–54. Title with dramatis personae on the verso extra.
> There appears to be a variant of this title in which '*Little*' is spelled correctly. (*Adler, P.&C.*)

82. K. Henry IV. | With | The Humours of | Sir John Falstaff. | A | Tragi-Comedy. | Written by Mr. W. Shakespear. | [O. monogrammic T.J. device] | London, | Printed the in Year 1710. [sic]

> Sm. 8vo. A–F, G². pn. (1)–100.
> Printed for T. Johnson at The Hague and also found in vol. ii, *A Collection of the Best English Plays*, 1712. (*B.M., B.H., S.*)

83. K. Henry IV. | With | the Humours of | Sir John Falstaff. | A | Tragi-Comedy, | By Mr. W. Shakespear.

| [O. monogrammic T.J. device] | London. | Printed for T. Johnson. | M.DCC.XXI.

> Sm. 8vo. A–E, F⁶. pn. (1)–92.
> The second edition of The Hague published plays.
> (*B.M., P.&C., Mich.*)

84. K. Henry IV | With | The Humours of | Sir. John Falstaff. | A | Tragi-Comedy. | = | Written by Mr. W. Shakespear. | = | [O. vase with flowers and leaves] | Dublin: | Printed by and for George Grierson, at the | Two Bibles in Essex-Street. 1723.

> Sm. 8vo. A–E, F⁵. pn. (1)–90.   (*H.N.P.*)

85. K. Henry IV. | With | The Humours of | Sir John Falstaff. | A | Tragi-Comedy | = | Written by Mr. W. Shakespear. | = | [O. small conventional] | ≡ | Dublin: | Printed by S. Powell. | For Thomas Moore, Bookseller, at | the Corner of Dirty-Lane in Dame-|street. MDCCXXXI.

> 12mo. A–C, D⁶. pn. (1)–(84), the last 2 pp. with Crampton's advertisement 'Plays Sold singly at a British Sixpence' including 'Hamblet alter'd by Mr. Pope' and 'Othello alter'd by Mr. Pope'.
> (*B.M.*)

86. The First Part of | Henry IV. | With the | Life and Death | of Henry Sirnamed Hot-spur. | = | By Mr. William Shakespear. | = | [O. SHO.] | London: | Printed for J. Tonson: And Sold by W. Feales, | at Rowe's Head, over-against Clement's-Inn Gate. | = | MDCCXXXII.

> 12mo. A–D. pn. 1–96. Headlines pp. 8, 32, 54, 78 printed 'first'.
> (*S.*)

87. The First Part of | Henry IV. | With the | Life and Death | of | Henry Sirnamed Hot-spur. | = | By Mr. William Shakespear. | = | [O. SHO.] | = | London: | [A] | MDCCXXXIV.

> 12mo. A–D. pn. (1)–96, exclusive of FO. plate (1728, 1714). CS. on p. (3).   (*B.M., B.H., S.*)

88. The First Part of | Henry IV. | With the | Life and

Death | of | Henry, Sirnamed Hotspur. | = | By Shake-
spear. | = | [O. Cupid's head supporting a basket of
flowers] | = | London: | [W. 4] MDCCXXXIV.

12mo. A–C, D⁶. pn. (1)–84, exclusive of rare F. by J. Smith,
with motto 'There lies Honour'.   (*B.M.*, *B.H.*)

89. The First Part of | Henry IV. | With the | Life
and Death | of | Henry, Sirnamed Hotspur. | = |
By Shakespear. | = | [O. book on bracket, supported
by a child's head] | = | London: | Printed in the Year
MDCCXXXVI.

12mo. A–C, D⁶. pn. (1)–84, exclusive of F. by J. Smith.
A reissue of Walker's, 1734, with a fresh title.   (*Folger*)

90. K. Henry IV. | with | the Humours of | Sir John
Falstaff. | A | Tragi-Comedy. | = | Written by Mr. W.
Shakespeare. | = | Collated with the oldest Copies, and
Corrected; with | Notes Explanatory and Critical. | By
Mr. Theobald. | ≡ | Dublin: | Printed by R. Reilly,
| Printed for John Smith, at the Philosophers Heads
on | the Blind-Key; and Abraham Bradley, | at the Two
Bibles in Dame's-Street. | = | M,DCC,XXXIX.

12mo. 2 ll.+A3–A13, B–D, E1. pn. (1)–(100), though the
numbered pages are (3)–98.
This was probably printed after *The Works* by the same publishers
in 1739.   (*Folger*)

ADVERTISED BUT NOT RECORDED

Henry IV, Pt. I.

G. Risk   .   .   .   . 1729 or A
G. Risk, G. Ewing, and W. Smith   .   .   . 1729 „

HENRY IV, PART II

91. The Sequel | of | Henry the Fourth: | with the
Humours of | Sir John Falstaffe, and Justice Shallow. |
As it is Acted by | His Majesty's Company of Come-
dians, | at the | Theatre-Royal in Drury-Lane | = |

Alter'd from Shakespear by the late Mr. Betterton. | ≡ | London: | Printed for W. Chetwood, at Cato's Head in Russel-|street, Covent Garden; and T. Jauncy, at the An-|gel without Temple-Bar. Price 1s. 6d | where may be had the Bishop of Canterbury's | Speech mention'd in this Play. Printed from the | Original. Price 6d. [N.D. *c.* 1720.]

> Narrow 4to. A–L, M1. pn. 8 pp. n.n.+(1)–82.
>
> (*P.&C., B.H.*)

92. The Second Part of | Henry IV. | Containing his Death: | and the | Coronation | of | King Henry V. | = | [O. SHO.] | = | London: | Printed for J. Tonson: And Sold by W. Feales, | at Rowe's Head, the Corner of Essex-Street in | the Strand. MDCCXXXIII.

> 12mo. A–D. pn. (1)–(96), including F. (1728, 1714). Dramatis personae on verso of title and last leaf blank. No advertisement leaf.
>
> (*B.H., S.*)

93. The Second Part of | Henry IV. | Containing his Death: | and the | Coronation | of | King Henry V. | = | By Mr. William Shakespear | = | [O. rabbit] | ≡ | London: | [A] | MDCCXXXIV.

> 12mo. A–D. pn. (1)–(96). Last leaf a blank. Exclusive of F. as used for 1728, 1714, which is a similar but smaller replica of the 1709, but in reverse. CS. on verso of title. Dramatis personae on A2 verso.
>
> (*B.M., B.H., S.*)

94. The Second Part of | Henry IV. | Containing his Death: | and the | Coronation | of | King Henry V. | = | By Shakespear. | = | [O. sun framed with cornu-copiae] | = | London: | [W. 10] MDCCXXXIV.

> 12mo. A–D. pn. 1–(96), but actually 98, pp. 73–4 being duplicated. Pagination includes F. similar to Tonson's, but re-engraved. Dramatis personae on verso of title with misprints 'Moreton' and 'Pang'. The last 3 leaves are occupied with Walker's vindication of his attitude and negotiations with Feales and Tonson, and terminates 'So that each Vol. of Tonson's may be called a Gallimaufry of Scraps and Nonsense'. In some copies these are lacking.
>
> (*B.M., B.H., S.*)

95. The Second Part of | Henry IV. | Containing his Death: | and the | Coronation | of | King Henry V. | = | By Shakespeare. | = | [O. Britannia facing right] | = | London: | Printed in the Year M.DCC.XXXV.

> 12mo. A–C, D⁹. pn. (1)–(90), but actually 92 as Walker's, 1734. Identical in every way except for title and dramatis personae on verso reset, with misprint 'Henry VI'. This was not issued with Walker's 3-leaf advertisement. Dramatis personae with misprints 'Humphery' and 'Pang'. (*S.*)

96. The Second Part of | Henry IV. | Containing his Death: | and the Coronation of King Henry V. | = | By Shakespeare, | = | [O.   ] | = | London: | Printed in the Year MDCCXXXVI.

> 12mo. A–C, D⁹. pn. (1)–(90).
> Printed by R. Walker. (*H.N.P.*)

HENRY V

97. The | Half-Pay Officers; | A | Comedy: | As it is Acted | By His Majesty's Servants. | = | Nullum est jam dictum, quod non dictum sit prius. | Terence. | = | The Second Edition. | = | [O. lyre and trumpets] | = | London: | Printed for A. Bettesworth, and W. Boreham, | in Pater-Noster-Row, T. Jauncy, at the Angel | without Temple-Bar, and J. Brotherton, and | W. Meadows in Cornhill. 1720. [Pr. *1s.*]

> 12mo, in sixes. A4, B–H. pn. 8 pp. n.n. + 1–(84) (B2 printed C3).
> Ascribed to C. Molloy. (*B.H.*)

98. King Henry | the Fifth. | or, The | Conquest of France, | By the English, | A | Tragedy. | As it is Acted at the | Theatre-Royal in Drury-Lane, | By His Majestys Servant's. | = | By Aaron Hill, Esq.; | ≡ | London: | Printed for W. Chetwood in the Passage to the Theatre-|Royal in Drury-Lane, and J. Watts at the Printing-|Office in Wild-Court near Lincoln's-Inn-Fields. 1723. | [Price 1s. 6d.]

> 8vo. A–E. pn. 16 pp. including the half-title n.n. + (1)–(64), the last 3 being 'Books sold by W. Chetwood'. Preface dated Dec. 5, 1723.

99. K. Henry V. | or, The | Conquest | of | France, | By the | English. | A | Tragedy. | = | By Aaron Hill, Esq; | = | Dublin: | Printed for George Grierson, in Essex-Street, | George Risk and George Ewing, in Dames-|Street, 1724.

8vo. A–D. pn. (1)–(64). 'A Catalogue of Plays' on the last p., has *Hamlet, Othello, Julius Caesar, All for Love, Henry IV. with the Humours, Revis'd by Mr. Dryden.*
A scarce edition. *(N.L.D., S.)*

100. The Life of | Henry V. | = | By William Shakespear. | = | [O. rabbit] | = | London: | [A] | MDCCXXXIV.

12mo. A–D. pn. (1)–96, excluding F. (1728, 1714). *(B.H., S.)*

101. The | Life | of | King Henry V. | = | By Shakespear | = | [O. woman's head in decorated roundel] | London: | [W. 10] M.DCC.XXXV.

12mo. A–C, D⁸. pn. (1)–88, exclusive of re-engraved F. by J. Smith. Dramatis personae spellings thus: 'Unkles', 'Burgandy', etc. *(S.)*

102. The | Life | of | King Henry V. | As it is Acted at the | Theatres. | = | By Shakespeare. | = | [O. tazza of flowers] | = | London: | Printed in the Year M.DCC.XXXV.

12mo. A–C, D⁸. pn. (1)–88. No F.: probably it should have one by J. Smith. A replica of Walker's and printed by him, only differing in title and dramatis personae, corrected, but with increased misspellings—Westmoreland, Cambrige, Flueilen, Ramures. *(S.)*

103. The | Life | of | King Henry V. | As it is Acted at the Theatres. | = | By Shakespear. | = | [O. bowl of fruit and flowers] | = | London: | Printed in the Year MDCCXXXVI.

12mo. A–C, D⁸. pn. (1)–88. May require F. Dramatis personae: the misspellings of the 1735 edition corrected except 'Westmoreland'.
Printed by Walker. *(H.N.P.)*

104. The | History | of | Henry | the | Fifth. | As it was Acted | At His Highness the Duke | of York's Theatre.

8vo. From T8 to Aa6. pn. (255)–364.
Being an excerpt from the 'Dramatic Works | of Roger Boyle, | Earl of Orrery. | = | —— Vol. I | = | London: | Printed for R. Dodsley, at Tully's Head, in Pall-|mall, MDCCXXXIX.' (*B.H.*)

ADVERTISED BUT NOT RECORDED

Henry V.

G. Risk, G. Ewing, W. Smith .   .   .   .   1729 or A.
J. Osborne. 8vo. .   .   .   .   .   .   1721 „
The Half Pay Officer, 1st edn.; only the 2nd edn. 1720 recorded.

HENRY VI, PART I

105. The | First Part | of | Henry VI. | = | By. Mr. William Shakespear. | = | [O. tazza floriated] | ≡ | London: | [B] | M.DCC.XXXV.

12mo. A–C, D⁶. pn. (1)–(84), exclusive of FO. F. (1728, 1714). Last leaf a blank.   (*B.M., B.H., S.*)

106. The | First Part | of | King Henry VI. | = | By Shakespear. | = | [O. tazza of fruit] | = | London: | [W. 11] MDCCXXXV.

12mo. A–C. pn. (1)–72, exclusive of FO. F. re-engraved in reverse.   (*B.M., B.H., S.*)

HENRY VI, PART II

107. Humfrey | Duke of | Gloucester. | A | Tragedy. | As it is Acted at the | Theatre-Royal in Drury-Lane | By | His Majesty's Servants. | = | By Mr. Philips. | = | The Second Edition: | With | Two Copies of Verses to the Authour. | [O. enclosed between 2 rules] | London, | Printed for J. Walthoe Jun. over-against the Royal-|Exchange in Cornhill; and J. Peele, at Lock's-Head | in Pater-noster-row. MDCCXXIII.

8vo. A⁴, A⁴, B–F, G⁴. pn. 16 pp. n.n.+(1)–(88).   (*P. &C.*)

108. Humfrey, | Duke of | Gloucester. | A | Tragedy. | As it is Acted at the | Theatre-Royal | in Drury-Lane, | By | His Majesty's Servants. | = | By Mr. Philips. | = | [O. angels trumpeting] | = | Dublin: | Printed by A. R. for J. Hyde, R. Gunne, R. Owen, | E. Dobson, P. Dugan and J. Leathly, 1723.

12mo, in sixes. A–F. pn. 10 pp. n.n.+(1)–(62).   (*P.&C., B.M.*)

109. Humfrey, | Duke of | Gloucester. | A | Tragedy. | As it is Acted at the | Theatre-Royal | in Drury Lane, | By His Majesty's Servants. | = | By Mr Philips. | = | [O.] | = | London, | Printed; And Sold by J. Roberts, near the Oxford-|Arms in Warwick-Lane, 1723.

8vo. ‡1, A⁴, B–G⁴. pn. 10 pp. n.n.+(1)–(88).   (*B.H.*)

110. The Second Part of | Henry | the Sixth. | With the Death of the | Good Duke Humphry. | A | Tragedy. | = | By Mr. William Shakespear. | = | [O. basket of fruit and flowers] | ≡ | London: | [B] | MDCCXXXIV.

12mo. A–C, D⁶. pn. (1)–84, exclusive of FO. F. (1728, 1714). p. 62 n. 63, 63 n. 62.
Some copies without stop to 'Sixth'.   (*B.M., B.H., S.*)

111. The | Second Part | of | King Henry VI. | With the Death of the | Good Duke Humphry. | = | By Shakespear. | = | [O. tazza of fruit] | = | London: | [W. 11] MDCCXXXV.

12mo. A–C, D⁶. pn. (1)–84, exclusive of FO. F. re-engraved in reverse by J. Smith.   (*B.M., B.H., S.*)

112. The Second Part of | King Henry VI. | with the Death of the | Good Duke Humphry. | As it is Acted at the | Theatres Royal. | = | By Shakespear. | = | [O. small bust enclosed in ornament] | = | London: Printed in the Year MDCCXXXVI.

12mo. A–C, D⁶. pn. (1)–84, exclusive of FO. plate re-engraved in reverse by J. Smith.
Printed by Walker, only differing from his edition in title-page and dramatis personae which is on the verso.   (*S.*)

ADVERTISED BUT NOT RECORDED

Henry VI.

Humphrey D. of Gloucester.
W. Feales .   .   .   .   1734 or A.

HENRY VI, PART III

113. An Historical Tragedy | of the | Civil Wars | in the Reign of | King Henry VI. | (Being a Sequel to the Tragedy of | Humfrey Duke of Gloucester: | And an Introduction to the Tragical History of | King Richard III.) | = | Alter'd from Shakespear, in the | Year 1720. | = | By Theo. Cibber. | = | Heu! quantum [&c. 2 lines]. Lucan. | = | London: | Printed for J. Walthoe, jun. in Cornhill; W. Chetwood, | in Russel-Street, Covent-Garden; and J. Stagg, in West-|minster-Hall: And Sold by J. Roberts, in Warwick-Lane. | Price 1s. 6d. [N.D. *c.*1722]

> Narrow 4to. A², B–I. pn. 4 pp. n.n.+(1)–(62). Actually, through pp. 55–6 being duplicated in numeration, should be (1)–(64).
> The B.H. copy lacks the advertisement leaf I4, which contains 'Books lately Printed'.
> The preface states: 'This Piece was finish'd above Two Years ago, and put into my Hands, to make what Use I thought fit' (possibly written by Chetwood). Rare.   (*B.H., B.M.*)

114. King Henry VI. | A | Tragedy. | As it is Acted at the | Theatre-Royal in Drury-Lane, | By His Majesty's Servants. | = | Altered from Shakespear, in the Year 1720, | By Theophilus Cibber. | = | Heu! quantum [&c. 2 lines]. Lucan. | = | The Second Edition | = | London: Printed for W. Chetwood at the Theatre-Royal | in Drury-Lane. 1724 (Price 1s. 6d.) Where may be had (just Publish'd) Henry the Fifth, | A Tragedy, written by Aaron Hill, Esq:

> Narrow 4to. ‡², B–I. pn. 4 pp. n.n.+(1)–(62). Last leaf contains books lately printed for Walthoe, Chetwood, and Stagg. Actually the pn. should be (1)–(64), as pp. 55–6 are repeated.
> This is a reissue of the first edition with 2 new leaves, being a fresh

title-page and a prologue spoken by Mr. Theophilus Cibber re-
placing the preface, with dramatis personae containing the cast, in
which Mr. Cibber Junior is Prince Edward. 'The Fortunes and
Misfortunes of the Famous Moll Flanders Price 5s.' finds place on
the advertisement leaf. (*Bod.*, *B.H.*, *P.&C.*)

115. The Third Part of | Henry | the | Sixth. | With
the Death of the | Duke of York. | = | By Mr. William
Shakespear. | = | [O. rabbit] | ≡ | London: | [A] |
MDCCXXXIV.

12mo. A–D. pn. (1)–96, exclusive of F. (1728, 1714).
(*B.M.*, *B.H.*, *S.*)

116. The | Third Part | of | King Henry VI. | With the
Death of the | Duke of York. | = | By Shakespear. | =
| [O. open book enclosed within ornament] | = |
London: | [W. 11] MDCCXXXV.

12mo. A–C, D⁴. pn. (1)–80, exclusive of re-engraved F. in reverse.
The headline to p. 26 is 'The Second Part of'. (*B.H.*, *B.M.*, *S.*)

117. The | Third Part | of | King Henry VI. | With
the Death of the | Duke of York. | = | By Shakespear. |
= | [O. urn foliated] | = | London: | Printed in the
Year MDCCXXXVI.

12mo. A–C, D⁴. pn. (1)–80, exclusive of F. engraved in reverse
probably by J. Smith.
Printed by Walker, and except for title and dramatis personae the
same as Walker's 1735 edition, with the same error p. 26. (*S.*)

ADVERTISED BUT NOT RECORDED

Henry VI.

R. Wellington. 4to . . . . . 1704 or A.
J. Osborn. 8vo. . . . . . 1721 „

HENRY VIII

118. The | Life | of | Henry VIII | = | By Mr.
William Shakespear. | = | [O. SHO.] | = | London: |
Printed for J. Tonson: And Sold by W. Feales, | at

Rowe's Head, over-against Clement's-Inn Gate. | = |
MDCCXXXII.

> 12mo. A–D. pn. (1)–(96) p. 9 n.n.; no F. issued with this.
> (*B.H., P.&C., S.*)

119. King Henry VIII. | A | Tragedy. | Containing the
following historical Relations. | I. The Execution of the
Duke of Buckingham. | II. The Trial and Divorce of
Q. Catherine. | III. The Fall of Cardinal Wolsey. |
IV. The marriage and Coronation of Anna Bullen. |
V The Christning of Q. Elizabeth. | With many other
remarkable Incidents. | = | As it is acted, with great
applause, at the | Theatres of London and Dublin. |
≡ | Dublin: | Printed by S. Powell in Crane-lane, | for
J. Leathley, in Dame-Street, T. Thornton | on College-
Green, A. Bradley at the Two Bibles, | and T. Moore
at Erasmus's Head, Booksellers in | Dame-Street.
MDCCXXXIV.

> Sm. 8vo. A⁸, B⁴, C⁸, D⁴, E⁸, F⁴. pn. 2 pp. n.n.+(1)–(70).
> A rare edition. (*Folger*)

120. The | Life and Death | of | King Henry | the |
Eighth. | = | By Mr. William Shakespear. | = | [O.
mask on banner] | = | London: | [A] | MDCCXXXIV.

> 12mo. A–D. pn. (1)–(96), exclusive of F. (1728, 1714). CS. on
> verso of title. In some copies p. 76 n. 74, and so where the Tp.,
> D12ᵛ, is upside down. (*B.M., B.H., S.*)

121. The Famous | History | of the | Life | of | King
Henry VIII. | With the Fall of | Cardinal Wolsey. | =
| By Shakespear. | = | [O. woman's head in foliated
roundel] | = | London: | [W. 7] MDCCXXXIV.

> 12mo. A–C, D⁸. pn. (1)–(88), exclusive of F. engraved in reverse.
> (*B.M., B.H., S.*)

122. The Famous | History | of the | Life | of | King
Henry VIII. | With the Fall of | Cardinal Wolsey. | = |

By Shakespeare. | = | [O. Britannia holding shield] | = | London: | Printed in the Year M.DCC.XXXV.

12mo. A–C, D⁸. pn. (1)–(88). Should probably have a F. extra. Except for title-page, identical with Walker's 1734 edition.   (*S.*)

123. The Famous | History | of the | Life | of | King Henry VIII. | With the Fall of | Cardinal Wolsey. | = | By Shakespear. | = | [O. bust on pedestal] | = | London: | Printed in the Year MDCCXXXVI.

12mo. A–C, D⁸. pn. (1)–88, exclusive of F. Identical with Walker's previous editions, except for title.   (*Folger*)

124. K. Henry VIII. | A | Tragedy. | Containing | The following Historical Relations: | I. The Execution of the Duke of Buckingham. | II. The Tryal and Divorce of Queen Catharine. | III. The Fall of Cardinal Wolsey. | IV. The Marriage and Coronation of Anne Bullen. | V. The Christening of Queen Elizabeth. | = | Written by Mr. W. Shakespeare. | = | Collated with the Oldest Copies, and Corrected; with | Notes Explanatory and Critical, | By Mr. Theobald. | ≡ | Dublin: | Printed by R. Reilly, | For Abraham Bradley, at the Two Bibles | in Dame's-Street, opposite Sycamore-Alley: | = | M.DCC.XXXIX.

‡1, A3 to A12, B–D, E³. pn. 2 pp. n.n.+(1)–(98). A reissue from vol. v of the *Works*, Theobald's 1739, Dublin, with the substitution of a fresh title in place of volume and contents titles. Otherwise the alphabet and pagination are identical. (*B.H.*)

KING JOHN

125. The | Life and Death | of | King John. | A | Tragedy. | = | By Mr. William Shakespear. | = | [O. basket of fruit and flowers] | ≡ | London: | [B] | MDCCXXXIV.

12mo. A–C. pn. (1)–72, exclusive of FO. plate (1728), after the 1714 of Kirkall's. TW. on half of last p. C4 is printed C2.   (*S.*)

126. The | Life and Death | of | King John. | A |
Tragedy. | By | Mr William Shakespear. | = | [O. lyre
and horns with sun] | = | London: | [C] | MDCCXXXIV.

> 12mo. A–C. pn. (1)–72, exclusive of FO. plate (1728) which was
> engraved after Kirkall's 1714. Dramatis personae and the last leaf
> reprinted, and on the last page the double peacock Tp. replaces
> Tonson's advertisement. A scarce state.
> [C], imprint as [A] but spaced –Pro–.   (*S*.)

127. The | Life and Death | of | King John. | A |
Tragedy. | = | By Shakespear. | = | [O. woman's head
in intaglio decorated] | = | London: | [W. 10]
MDCCXXXV.

> 12mo. A–C. pn. (1)–72, exclusive of F. engraved in reverse after
> FO.   (*B.M., B.H.*)

128. The | Life and Death. | of | King John. | A |
Tragedy. | By Shakespear. | = | [O.] | = | London: |
Printed in the Year MDCCXXXVI.

> 12mo. A–C. pn. (1)–72. Possibly may require a F.
> Printed by R. Walker.   (*H.N.P.*)

KING LEAR

129. The | History | of | King | Lear. | Acted at the |
Queens Theatre. | = | Revived with Alterations. | = |
By N. Tate. | = | London, | Printed for Rich. Welling-
ton, at the Dolphin and Crown in St. Paul's | Church-
Yard, and E. Rumbold at the Post House, Covent
Garden; and | Tho. Osborne at Grays-Inn, near the
Walks. | = | There is newly Published, Mr Glanvil's
Discourse [&c. 8 lines] | Where Gentlemen and Ladies
may have all sorts of Novels and Plays. [N.D. *c.* 1702.]

> 4to. A–D, F–I². pn. (1)–60. p. 14 n. 41.
> Mrs. Behn's plays in 2 volumes are advertised, that were published
> in 1702. So this is not earlier.   (*B.H., B.M., Adler*)

130. The | History | of | King Lear, | Acted at the |
Queens Theatre. | = | Revived with Alterations. | =

| By N. Tate. | = | London: Printed for Richard Wellington, at the Dolphin and Crown in | St. Paul's Church-Yard. 1712. | = | This Day is Published; The Art of Pleasing in Conversation [&c. 19 lines] | Where Gentlemen and Ladies may have all sorts of Novels and Plays.

> 4to. A–G, H². pn. (1)–60. The type entirely reset from the 1700 edition. *(B.H., B.M., Adler)*

131. King | Lear, | A | Tragedy. | = | [O. billing doves] | = | London: | Printed by J. Darby for M. P. and sold by A. | Bettesworth in Pater-noster-row, and F. Clay | without Temple-bar. M.DCC.XXIII. | (Price 1s.)

> 12mo, in sixes. A–G. pn. (1)–84. F. by Dandridge—Van der Gucht extra. *(B.H., S.)*

132. The | History | of | King Lear. | = | Revived with Alterations. | = | By N. Tate. | = | [O. bear and clubs] | = | Dublin: | Printed by Pressick Rider, and Tho- | mas Harbin, for William Smith, at the Dutchess's Head in Dames-Street, | MDCCXXIV.

> 12mo. A–F in sixes, G⁴. 80 pp. 'Books printed' on last p. *(P.&C.)*

133. The | History | of | King Lear: | A | Tragedy, | As it is now Acted at the | King's Theatre. | = | Reviv'd with Alterations. | = | By N. Tate. | = | [O. scrolly decoration] | = | London: | Printed in the Year, 1729.

> 12mo, in sixes. A–F. pn. (1)–(72). *(B.H.)*

134. The History of King Lear. | = | Revived with Alterations. | = | By N. Tate. | = | [O. hive and bees] | = | Dublin: | Printed by S. Powell, | For William Smith, at the Hercules, in Dame's- | street. MDCCXXXIII.

> 12mo. A–C, D⁶. pn. (1)–(84). The last 5 pp. consist of catalogue, 'Books, Poems and Plays Printed for G. Risk, G. Ewing, and W. Smith, wherein' Shakespear's *Works*, 8 vols., 12mo, pr. '1*l*.8*s*.' appear. *(B.M., P.&C.)*

135. The | Life and Death | of | King Lear. | = | By Mr. William Shakespear. | = | [O. SHO.] | = | London : | [A] | MDCCXXXIV.

> 12mo. A–D. pn. (1)–(96), the last 4 pp. being blank, p. 56 n. 46. Excluding LDG. F. (1728, 1714). CS. on p. 92. About half the copies examined lack the blank pages. (*B.M., S.*)

136. The | History | of | King Lear, | and | His Three Daughters : | A | Tragedy, | As it is acted at the Theatres. | = | By Shakespear. | = | With alterations by N. Tate. | = | London : | [W. 8] M.DCC.XXXIV.

> 12mo. A⁴, B, C, D⁶. pn. 8 pp. n.n.+(1)–(60), including LDG. F. re-engraved by Smith. D6 contains the epilogue. (*B.M., B.H., S.*)

137. The | History | of | King Lear, | A | Tragedy. | Acted at the | King's Theatre. | = | Reviv'd with Alterations, | = | By N. Tate. | = | London ; | Printed for W. Feales at Rowe's-Head over-|against St. Clement's Church in the Strand. | MDCCXXXVI.

> 12mo, in sixes. A–F. pn. (1)–72, F. by Van der Gucht extra. Last p. blank.
> One of the series of plays advertised by Feales in 1736. (*H.N.P.*)

138. The | History | of | King Lear. | = | Written by Mr. W. Shakespeare | = | Collated with the Oldest Copies and Corrected : With | Notes Explanatory and Critical, | By Mr Theobald. | = Dublin : | Printed by R. Reilly, | Printed for John Smith, at the Philosophers Heads on | the Blind-Key ; And Abraham Bradley, | at the Two Bibles in Dame's-Street | = | M.DCC.XXXIX.

> 12mo. ‡², A–D, E⁸. pn. 4 pp. n.n.+(1)–(112).
> This is a reprint for separate sale of the play in the Dublin edition, 1739, of the *Works*, in which it occupies E4 to I, pp. (99)–(212), vol. v; an extra leaf was added with the above title; the catchword 'Timon' on p. 111, and p. 211 in the set. (*B.M.*)

King Lear.

T. Astley	. . . .	.	1728 or A.
G. Risk	. . . .	.	1729 ,,
J. Poulson and the Wellingtons		.	1731; also Tate's version.
W. Feales	. . . .	.	1734 or A.
W. Smith, Dublin	. .	.	1725 ,,

KING RICHARD II

139. The | Tragedy | of | King Richard the II; | As it is Acted at the | Theatre in Lincoln's-Inn-Fields. | = | Alter'd from Shakespear, | By Mr. Theobald. | = | Quis Talia [3 lines]. Virg. | ≡ | London: | Printed for G. Strahan at the Golden Ball in | Corn hill, W. Mears without Temple Bar, | T. Meighan in Drury Lane, B. Barker in | Westminster Hall, and Sold by J. Morphew near | Stationers Hall, 1720. (Price 1s. 6d.)

Narrow 4to. a, aa–bb, B–H, I². pn. 24 pp. n.n.+(1)–60.
(*Bod., B.M., Mich.*)

140. The | Life and Death | of | Richard | the | Second. | = | By Mr. William Shakespear. | = | [O. rabbit.] | ≡ | London: | [A] | MDCCXXXIV.

12mo. A–C, D⁶. pn. (1)–84, exclusive of LDG. F. (1728, 1714). pp. 41 and 46 n. on inner margin. (*S.*)

141. The | Life and Death | of | Richard II. | = | By Shakespear. | = | [O. pelican in oval] | = | London: | [W. 11] MDCCXXXV.

12mo. A–C, D⁶. pn. (1)–84, excluding the F. engraved in reverse.
(*B.H., B.M.*)

142. The | Life and Death | of | Richard II. | = | By Shakespeare. | = | [O. Gorgon's head] | = | London: Printed in the Year M.DCC.XXXV.

12mo. A–C, D⁶. pn. (1)–84, excluding the F. of the abdication scene in reverse. Walker's printing with a fresh title. (*H.N.P.*)

143. The | Life and Death | of Richard II. | As it is Acted at the | Theatres. | = | By Shakespear. | = | [O.] | = | London: | Printed in the Year MDCCXXXVI.

12mo. A–C, D⁶. pn. (1)–84.
Printed by R. Walker.   (*H.N.P.*)

ADVERTISED BUT NOT RECORDED

K. Richard II.
    R. Wellington. 4to.   .   .   .   .   .   1705 or A.

KING RICHARD III

144. The | Tragical History | of | King Richard III. | As it is Acted at the | Theatre Royal. | = | By C. Cibber. | = | — Domestica Facta. | = | London, | Printed for B. Lintott at the Middle Temple-Gate, in Eleet [sic]-street, and | A. Bettesworth at the Red-Lyon on London-Bridge. | = | [Advertisement of 9 lines, novels, &c.] [N.D. *c.* 1700.]

Sm. 4to. A–H. pn. 8 pp. n.n.+1–56.   (*Mich.*)

145. The Tragical | History | of | King Richard the Third. | containing | The Distresses and Death of | King Henry the Sixth. | The Artful Acquisition | of the Crown by King | Richard. | The Cruel Murder of | young King Edward | the Fifth, and his Bro-|ther in the Tower. | |||. The Landing of the Earl | of Richmond, and the | Death of King Rich-|ard in the memorable | Battle of Bosworth-Field: | Being the last that was | fought between the | Houses of York and | Lancaster. | With many other Historical Passages. | = As it is now Acted at the Theatre-|Royal in Drury-Lane. | = | Reviv'd, with Alterations, by Mr. Cibber. | = | — Domestica Facta. | = | London: | Printed for W. Mears, at the Lamb, and J. Browne, | at the Black-Swan without Temple-Bar, and W. Chet-|wood, at

Cato's Head in Russell-Court, near the | Theatre-Royal, MDCCXVIII.

> 12mo, in sixes. A–F. pn. (1)–(72), including F. by Kirkall.
> pp. 49–60 n. 61–72, and from thence 61–(72).   (*B.M., B.H., S.*)

146. The | Life and Death | of | Richard III. | With the Landing of the | Earl of Richmond, | and the | Battle at Bosworth-Field. | = | By Mr. William Shakespear. | = | [O. SHO.] | ≡ | London: | [A] | MDCCXXXIV.

> 12mo. A–D. pn. (1)–96, FO. plate extra, p. 61 n. inner margin. Headline on p. 5, reads 'Ricaard'. Mercury's Head Tp. and Trophy Hp. Initial N (A2) surmounted by basket of fruit.   (*S.*)

147. The | Life and Death | of | Richard III. | With the Landing of the | Earl of Richmond, | and the | Battle at Bosworth-Field. | = | By Mr. William Shakespear, | = | [O. basket of fruit] | ≡ | London: | [B] | MDCCXXXIV.

> 12mo. A–D. pn. (1)–96. FO. plate extra (1728, 1714). Conventional Hp., small capital N (A2) decorated with daisies. Basket of fruit Tp. Text reset.   (*B.H., S.*)

148. The | Life and Death | of Richard III. | With the Landing of the | Earl of Richmond, | and the | Battle at Bosworth-Field. | = | By Mr. William Shakespear. | = | [O. basket of fruit] | ≡ | London: | [B] | MDCCXXXIV.

> 12mo. A–D. pn. (1)–96. FO. plate extra. TW. advertisement replaces Tp., and common ornament as Hp. Initial N (A2) framed with cupids. Text again reset.   (*S.*)

149. The | Life and Death | of | Richard III. | A | Tragedy. | with the Landing of the | Earl of Richmond, | and the | Battle at Bosworth Field. | Being the Last between the Houses of | Lancaster and York. | = | By Shakespear. | = | London: | [W. 4] MDCCXXXIV. | (Price 4d. with the Frontispiece.)

> 12mo. A–D. pn. (1)–96, exclusive of FO. F. done in reverse by J. Smith. Mask and birds Hp. to p. 3. Large capital N in scenery block. A2, A3, A4, A5, D3 printed A, A4, A3, A4, D2.
>   (*B.M., B.H., S.*)

150. The Life and Death | of | Richard III. | [as

the previous one of Walker's] | London: | [W. 3]
MDCCXXXIV. | (Price 4d. with the Frontispiece.)

> 12mo. A–D. pn. (1)–96, exclusive of F. by J. Smith after FO.
> Classic scroll Hp. to p. 3 and small capital N in block with basket
> of flowers. Title reset and most of the text. Sheets A and B were
> entirely reprinted. (*S.*)

151. The Tragical | History | of | King Richard III. |
Containing, |

The Distresses and Death of	King Henry the Sixth.	The Artful Acquisition	of the Crown by King Richard.	The Cruel Murder of young	King Edward the	Fifth and his Brother	in the Tower.		The Landing of the Earl of	Richmond and the Death of King Rich-|ard in the memorable	Battle of Bosworth Field:	Being the last that was	fought between the	Houses of York and Lancaster.	

With many other Historical Passages. | = | As it is now
Acted at the Theatre-|Royal in Drury-Lane. | = |
Reviv'd with Alterations, by Mr. Cibber. | = | —
Domestica Facta. | = | London: | Printed for W. Feales,
at Rowe's Head, the Corner of | Essex-street in the
Strand; R. Wellington, at the | Dolphin and Crown
near Temple-bar; J. Welling-|ton; and A. Bettesworth
and F. Clay in | trust for B. Wellington. MDCCXXXIV.

> 12mo, in sixes. ‡5, B–F. pn. 5 pp. n.n.+8–84. There is a
> gap in the pagination, the numbers jumping from 48 to 61.
> Probably should have a F. (*B.H.*)

152. The Tragical | History | of | King Richard III. |
containing |

The Distresses and Death of King Henry the Sixth.	The Artful Acquisition	of the Crown by King Richard.	The Cruel Murder of	young King Edward	the Fifth, and his Bro-|ther in the Tower.		The Landing of the Earl	of Richmond, and the	Death of King Rich-|ard in the memorable	Battle of Bosworth-Field:	Being the last that was	fought between the	Houses of York and	Lancaster.	

With many other Historical Passages. | As it is now
Acted at the Theatre-|Royal in Drury-Lane. | = |
Reviv'd with Alterations, by Mr Cibber. | = | —
Domestica Facta. | = | London: | Printed for W. Feales,
at Rowe's Head the Corner of | Essex-Street in the
Strand; R. Wellington, at the | Dolphin and Crown
near Temple-Bar; J. Wellington; | and A. Bettes-
worth, and F. Clay, in Trust for B. Wellington. | = |
M.DCC.XXXVI.

> 12mo, in sixes. A–F. 72 pp., but misnumbered from p. 48. This
> includes a F. or a blank for pp. 1–2.
> Issued again the same year with differently spaced title.

153. The Tragical | History | of King Richard III. |
containing |

The Distresses and Death of	King Henry the Sixth.	The Artful Acquisition of the Crown by King Richard.	The Cruel Murder of Young	King Edward the	Fifth, and his Brother	in the Tower.		The Landing of the Earl of	Richmond, and the	Death of King Ri-|chard in the memo-|rable Battle of Bosworth-|Field: Being the last that	was fought between the	Houses of York and Lan-|caster.	

With many other Historical Passages. | As it is now
Acted at the Theatre-|Royal in Drury-Lane. | = |
Reviv'd with Alterations, by Mr. Cibber. | = | —
Domestica Facta. | = | London: | Printed for W. Feales,
at Rowe's Head the Corner of | Essex-Street in the
Strand; R. Wellington at the | Dolphin and Crown
near Temple-Bar; J. Welling-|ton; and A. Bettes-
worth, and F. Clay, in | Trust for B. Wellington. | = |
MDCCXXXVI.

> 12mo, in sixes. A–F. pn. 7 pp. n.n. including F.+8–48+61–84.
> (*B.H.*)

154. The Tragical | History | of | King Richard III. |
As it is Acted at the Theatre-|Royal in Drury-Lane. |

Containing | The Distresses and Death of King Henry
the Sixth. | The Artful Acquisition of the Crown by
King Richard. | The Cruel Murder of young King
Edward the Fifth, | and his Brother in the Tower. |
The Landing of the Earl of Richmond, and the
Death | of King Richard in the memorable Battle
of Bos-|worth-Field: Being the last that was fought
between | the Houses of York and Lancaster. | With many
other Historical Passages. | = | Alter'd by Mr Cibber
| = | — Domestica Facta. | = | London: | Printed for
J. Tonson, and J. Watts, and | sold by W. Feales, the
Corner | of Essex-street in the Strand. | = | MDCCXXXVI.

12mo. A–C. pn. (1)–(72), including the scarce F. of the presenta-
tion of the Crown to Henry VII on Bosworth Field.   (*P.&C.*)

ADVERTISED BUT NOT RECORDED

K. Richard III.

R. Wellington. 4to   .   .   .   .   . 1704 or A.
Tonson. 4to. An excerpt from Cibber's works . 1721

LOCRINE

155. The | Tragedy | of | Locrine, | The | Eldest Son |
of | King Brutus. | = | By Mr. William Shakespear. |
= | [O. marigold] | = | London; [A] | MDCCXXXIV.

12mo. A–B, C⁶. pn. (1)–(60), exclusive of F. (1728, 1714). T.W.
on last p.   (*B.M., B.H., S.*)

156. The | Tragedy | of | Locrine, | The | Eldest Son |
of | King Brutus. | = | By Shakespear. | = | [O.
woman's head in decorated roundel] | = | London: |
[W. 8] MDCCXXXIV.

12mo. A, B, C⁶. pn. (1)–(60), exclusive of F. re-engraved probably
by J. Smith. Last leaf has Walker's 'Advertisement | As the Plays
printed by Tonson and his Accomplices, are from erroneous
Editions [etc.].' Paging irregular, pp. 25–6 omitted, and 49–50
repeated.   (*B.M., B.H., S.*)

157. The | Tragedy | of | Locrine, | The | Eldest Son | of | King Brutus. | = | By Shakespear. | = | [O. woman's head in decorated roundel] | = | London: | [W. 8] MDCCXXXIV.

> 12mo. A, B, C⁵. pn. (1)–58, exclusive of re-engraved F. Published without the advertisement and in this case there is a stub to C, generally the state in Walker's vol. iv. pp. 25–6 are missing, but 49–50 are repeated. (*S.*)

LONDON PRODIGAL

158. The | London | Prodigal. | A | comedy. | = | By Mr. William Shakespear. | = | [O. cornucopiae and birds] | ≡ | London: | [B] | MDCCXXXIV.

> 12mo. A¹², E¹², F⁶. pn. (1)–24+97–(132), exclusive of FO. plate (1728, 1714). A remarkable example of source of text, the last 34 pp. (97–130) correspond in numeration and alphabet with Pope's 1728 edition, though the type is entirely reset. p. (131) CL. (*B.M., B.H., S.*)

159. The | London | Prodigal. | A | Comedy. | = | By Shakespear. | = | [O. intaglioed woman's head] | = | London: | [W. 4] MDCCXXXIV.

> 12mo. ‡¹, B¹², B¹². pn. 4 pp. n.n.+(1)–48. F. re-engraved by J. Smith extra. Of the first gathering B4 printed A4. (*B.M., B.H., S.*)

LOVES LABOUR'S LOST [sic. 4to and folio.]

160. Love's | Labour's Lost. | A | Comedy. | = | By Mr. William Shakespear. | = | [O. floreated tazza] | ≡ | London: | [A] | MDCCXXXV.

> 12mo. A–C, D⁶. pn. (1)–84, exclusive of LDG. plate (1728, 1714). Headline to p. 81, 'Labour'. p. 34 n. 36; p. 35 n. 33. (*B.M., B.H., S.*)

161. Love's | Labour's Lost. | A | Comedy. | = | By Shakespear. | = | [O. pelican framed in oval] | = | London: | [W. 11] MDCCXXXV.

> 12mo. A–C. pn. (1)–72, exclusive of F. (*B.M., B.H.*)

MACBETH

162. Macbeth, | A | Tragedy. | With all the | Altera-
tions, | Amendments, | Additions, | and | New Songs. |
As it is now Acted at the | Queens-Theatre. | = |
London: | Printed for J. Tonson: And Sold by John
Phillips at the Black | Bull over-against the Royal
Exchange in Cornhill. 1710.

> 4to. A², B–G, H². pn. 4 pp. n.n.+1–52. The fifth edition, catch-
> word 'Mac' to dramatis personae. *(Adler, Dobell)*

163. Macbeth, 1710.

> Title and imprint similar to the preceding but text entirely reset.
> No catchword, and p. 1 'Opligd' instead of 'Oblig'd'. Dramatis
> personae similar, with Wilks as Macduff and Betterton as Macbeth.
> The sixth edition. The collation is the same. *(Adler)*

164. The | Tragedy | of Macbeth. | Writen by Mr. W.
Shakespear. | [O. monogrammic T. J.] | London, |
Printed in the Year 1711.

> Sm. 8vo. A–E, F². pn. (1)–(84).
> Printed for T. Johnson at The Hague, and also forming part of
> vol. i *A Collection of the Best English Plays*, 1711. *(B.M., S.)*

165. The | Tragedy | of | Macbeth. | Writen [sic] by
Mr. W. Shakespear. | [O. monogrammic T. J.] |
London, | Printed for the Company. [N.D. *c.* 1720.]

> Sm. 8vo. A–D, E⁶. pn. (1)–76.
> From the same press that printed the 1711 edition for T. Johnson
> at The Hague. Similar text but entirely reset. The headline to
> p. 71 reads 'Mackbet'. A scarce edition. *(B.H., S.)*

166. The | Tragedy | of | Macbeth. | = | Written by
Mr. W. Shakespear. | = | [O.] | = | Dublin: | Printed
for George Ewing, Bookseller, at the | Sign of the
Angel and Bible in Dames-Street. | 1723.

> 12mo. A–B, C¹⁰. 68 pp. p. 67 contains list of plays sold by George
> Ewing, including *Julius Caesar*, *Hamlet*, and *Othello*; p. 68 is
> a blank.

167. Macbeth; | A | Tragedy, | As it is now Acted by His Ma- | jesty's Servants. | = | Written by | William Shakespear. | = | [O. rabbit] | = | London, | Printed for J. Tonson; and also for J. Darby, | A. Bettesworth, and F. Clay, in Trust | for Richard, James, and Bethel Wel-|lington. M.DCC.XXIX.

> 12mo, in sixes. A to G. pn. (1)–(84). The last leaf contains 'Books printed (etc)' for J. Tonson, in which the edition of Pope's, 6 vols., 4to, and 9 vols., 12mo, are advertised. *(B.H., S.)*

168. Macbeth: | A | Tragedy; | As it is now Acted at the New Theatre | of | Edinburgh. | = | Written by Mr. Shakespear, with | Alterations by Mr. Tate. | = | [O. two common cuts] | = | Edinburgh: | Printed by T. and W. Ruddimans for Allan | Ramsay, and Sold at his Shop, 1731. | Price One Shilling.

> 12mo, in sixes. ‡¹, A–F. pn. 2 pp. n.n.+1–72.
> Very scarce: a copy at Sotheby's May in 1901 brought £30. *(B.H.)*

169. The | Tragedy | of | Macbeth. | = | By Mr. William Shakespear. | = | To which are added, | All the Original Songs. | Never Printed in any of the former Editions. | = | [O. SHO.] | ≡ | London: | [A] | MDCCXXXIV.

> 12mo. A–C. pn. (1)–(72), exclusive of LDG. plate (1728, 1714). CS. on verso of title. The songs occupy the last 2 leaves. *(B.M., B.H., S.)*

170. Macbeth; | A Tragedy. | As it is Acted at the | Theatres. | = | By Shakespear. | = | [O. intaglio woman's head decorated] | = | London: | [W. 4] MDCCXXXIV.

> 12mo. A–C+2 leaves of songs. pn. (1)–(76), including F. by LDG. re-engraved by J. Smith. pp. 71–2 are blank. *(B.M., B.H.)*

171. Macbeth. | A | Tragedy. | As it was Acted at the | Theatre-Royal. | = | By Shakespeare. [O. small Neptune] | = | London: | Printed in the Year MDCCXXXV.

> 12mo. A, B, C¹¹, ‡². pn. (1)–(74), including LDG. F. re-engraved by Smith. The last 4 pp. contain the songs.
> Walker's printing with a fresh title. *(H.N.P.)*

172. Macbeth. | A | Tragedy. | As it is now Acted | By His Majesty's Servants. | = | Written by William Shakespear. | = | [O. Britannia holding shield on left] | = | London: | Printed for W. Feales, at Rowe's-Head, over-|against St. Clement's Church in the Strand. | = | M.DCC.XXXVI.

> 12mo. A–G in sixes. pn. (1)–(84), exclusive of F. by ⌐DG. (1728, 1714). Last leaf contains 'Books printed for J Tonson' and 'Books Sold by J Darby (etc)'. *(Adler)*

173. The | Tragedy | of | Macbeth. | = | Written by Mr. W. Shakespeare. | = | Collated with the Oldest Copies, and Corrected; with | Notes Explanatory and Critical, | by Mr. Theobald. | = | Dublin: | Printed by M. Rhames, | For J. Smith, Bookseller, at the Philoso-|phers Heads on the Blind-Quay. And | Abraham Bradley, at the | Two Bibles in Dame's-Street. | = | M.DCC.XXXIX.

> 12mo. A–C, D⁸. pn. (1)–88.
> A separate issue of the play as printed in the 1739 Dublin of Theobald's, in which it occupies Q8 to U3, pp. (371)–458.
> *(Folger)*

ADVERTISED BUT NOT RECORDED

Macbeth.

R. Wellington. 4to.	.	.	.	. 1704 or A.
J. Darby for M. Wellington	.	.	.	. 1718 „
J. Poulson	.	.	.	. 1731 „
W. Feales	.	.	.	. 1734 „
G. Risk, G. Ewing, and W. Smith	.	.	.	. 1729 „

MEASURE FOR MEASURE

174. Measure for Measure. | or | Beauty | the | Best Advocate. | As it is acted | at the Theatre in Lincolns-Inn-Fields. | = | Written Originally by Mr. Shake-spear: | And now very much Alter'd; With Additions | of several Entertainments of Musick. | = | London: | Printed for D. Brown, at the Black Swan without

Temple-Bar, and | R. Parker at the Unicorn under the
Royal-Exchange | in Cornhill. 1700.

> 4to. A–G. pn. 8 pp. n.n.+1–48, including a half-title with a list
> of books printed on its obverse. The last 2 numbered pp., 47, 48,
> are misnumbered 39, 84. The alterations by Charles Gildon.
>
> (*Dobell*)

175. Measure | for Measure. | A | Comedy. | As it is
Acted at the | Theatre-Royal | In Lincolns-Inn-Fields.
| = | Written by Mr. W. Shakespear. | = | London:
| Printed for J. Tonson in the Strand; and | Sold by
W. Chetwood at Cato's Head in | Russel-street,
Covent-Garden. 1722.

> 12mo. A–C, D⁶. pn. (1)–84. No F. With similar instructions to
> Walker's edition, 1734, as regards acting elisions and additions.
> Dramatis personae, with Mr. Quin as the Duke.
>
> (*B.H., P.&C., S.*)

176. Measure | for | Measure. | = | By Mr. William
Shakespear. | = | [O. fleur-de-lis ornamented] | = |
London: | [A] | MDCCXXXIV.

> 12mo. A–C, D⁶. pn. (1)–(84), exclusive of LDG. plate (1728,
> 1714). CL. on recto A2. Text, &c., not as Pope's.
>
> (*B.M., B.H., S.*)

177. Measure | for | Measure. | A | Comedy: | As it
is Acted at the | Theatres. | = | By Shakespear. | = |
[O. billing doves] | = | London: | [W. 3] MDCCXXXIV.
| (Price 4d. with the Frontispiece.

> 12mo. A–C. pn. (1)–72, exclusive of rare plate, depicting the
> Friar, Provost, and Isabella. At the foot of dramatis personae, 'N.B.
> The Lines thus marked ' (by reason of the Length of the Play) are
> left out in the Performance'; and on the last page, 'These last eight
> Lines were added upon the Revival'. (*B.M., B.H.*)

178. Measure | for | Measure. | A | Comedy. | As it is
Acted at the | Theatres. | = | By Shakespeare. | = |
[O. vase of fruit.] | = | London: | Printed in the Year
M.DCC.XXXV.

> 12mo. A–C. pn. (1)–72, exclusive of plate and in all other par-
> ticulars as Walker's edition, 1734. (*S.*)

179. Measure | for | Measure. | A | Comedy: | As it is
Acted at the | Theatres. | = | By Shakespear. | = | [O.
basket of flowers] | = | London: | Printed in the Year
MDCCXXXVI.

> 12mo. A–C. pn. (1)–72, exclusive of F.
> Walker's issue with a fresh title.   (*H.N.P.*)

ADVERTISED BUT NOT RECORDED

Measure for Measure.

> J. Osborn. 12mo.   .   .   .   .   .   1721 or A.
> T. Astley .   .   .   .   1728 „

MERCHANT OF VENICE

180. The | Jew of Venice. | A | Comedy. | As it is Acted
at the | Theatre in Little-Lincolns-Inn-Fields, | By |
His Majesty's Servants. | = | London, | Printed for
Ber. Lintott at the Post-House | in the Middle Temple-
Gate, Fleet-street, 1701. | = | Tomorrow will be
Published [&c. 5 lines].

> 4to. A–G. pn. 8 pp. n.n.+(1) [*sic*]–(48), including the half-title.
> On the last page, 'Books and Plays Sold by Ber. Lintott', occur the
> following titles: *Titus Andronicus, Henry the Sixth, Timon of Athens,
> Troilus and Cressida, Anthony and Cleopatra, Mackbeth, Hamlet
> Prince of Denmark*, and *The Tempest.*   (*Adler, P.&C.*)

181. The Jew | of | Venice. | A | Comedy. | Written
Originaly | By Mr. Wm. Shakespear. | Now altered &
very much improved, | By the Hon. M. Granville. |
[O. monogrammic T. J.] | Printed for T. Johnson, |
Bookseller at the Hague. | = | M.DCC.XI.

> Sm. 8vo. A–D, E². pn. (1)–(68). p. 44 n. 42.
> Published separately, and also forming a portion of vol. ii, *A Col-
> lection of the Best English Plays*, 1712.   (*B.M., S.*)

182. The | Jew of Venice: | A | Comedy. | As it is
Acted at the | Theatre | in | Little-Lincolns-Inn-Fields.

| By | His Majesty's Servants. | ≡ | London : | Printed for Benj. Tooke, and Bern. Lintott, | 1713.

> 8vo. L6 to L8, M–P. pp. (171)–(240).
> An excerpt from Granville's (Lansdowne) plays, 1713.   (*P. & C.*)

183. The | Jew of Venice: | A | Comedy, | As it is Acted at the | Theatre | in | Little Lincoln's-Inn-Fields, | By | His Majesty's Servants. | ≡ | London: | Printed for Bernard Lintot, and for B. Motte, at the Middle-Temple-Gate; and sold by Henry | Lintot, over against St. Dunstan's Church in Fleet-|street; W. Feals, at Row's Head over against | Clement's Inn Gate. 1732.

> 12mo. G11 to K6. pn. (165)–(228). F. of the Casket scene extra.
> p. 174 n. 175, p. 214 n. 14.
> An excerpt from 'Four Plays of—Lord Lansdowne'. W. Feales, 1732.   (*S.*)

184. [A line of O.] | The | Jew of Venice. | A | Comedy. | [O. line.] (N.D. 1732.)

> Large 4to. S to Ff3. pn. (129)–(221).
> An excerpt from 'The Genuine | Works | in | Verse and Prose, | of the Right Honourable | George Granville, | Lord Lansdowne. | Vol. II. | London: | Printed for J. Walthoe, over-against the | Royal-Exchange, in Cornhill. | ≡ | MDCCXXXII.'   (*B.H.*)

185. The | Merchant | of | Venice. | = | By Mr. William Shakespear. | = | [O. arum spray] | = | London; | [A] | MDCCXXXIV.

> 12mo. A–C. pn. (1)–72, exclusive of FO. plate (1728, 1714).
>   (*B.M., B.H., S.*)

186. The | Merchant | of | Venice. | = | By Shakespear. | = | [O. woman's head in floriated roundel] | = | London: | [W. 10] M.DCC.XXXV.

> 12mo. A–C. pn. (1)–72, exclusive of FO. plate re-engraved in reverse by J. Smith.   (*B.M., B.H., S.*)

187. The | Merchant | of | Venice, | = | By Shake-

speare. | = | [O. rising sun on a bracket] | = | London:
| Printed in the Year M.DCC.XXXV.

> 12mo. A–C. pn. (1)–72, as Walker's, 1735, except title and
> dramatis personae.   (*S.*)

188. = | The | Jew of Venice. | A | Comedy. | =
(1736).

> 12mo. F6 to I5ʳ. pn. (107)–178.
> Being an excerpt from 'The Genuine | Works | in Verse and Prose, |
> Of the Right Honourable | George Granville, | Lord Lansdowne. |
> = | Vol III. | = | [O. tazza of flowers] | London: | Printed for
> J. Walthoe, over against the | Royal-Exchange in Cornhill | = |
> M.DCC.XXXVI.
> N.B. Vol. i of this edition 'Printed for J. & R. Tonson'.   (*B.M.*)

ADVERTISED BUT NOT RECORDED

Merchant of Venice.
> *Jew of Venice*, W. Feales   .   .   .   .   1734 or A.

MERRY WIVES OF WINDSOR

189. The | Comical Gallant: or the | Amours of Sir
John Falstaffe. | A | Comedy. | As it is Acted at the |
Theatre Royal in Drury Lane. | By his Majesty's
Servants. | = | By Mr. Dennis | = | To which is added,
| A large Account of the Taste in | Poetry, and the
Causes of the | Degeneracy of it. | = | London, |
Printed, and Sold by A. Baldwin, near the Oxford
Arms in War-|wicklane. 1702.

> 4to. A, a, B–F, G⁵. pn. 16 pp. n.n.+1–(50).
> The epistle dedicatory to the Honourable George Granville, Esq.
> covers 13 pp., and is well worth perusal.   (*B.H.*, *Dobell.*)

190. The | Merry Wives | of | Windsor; | With the |
Amours | of | Sir John Falstaff. | A | Comedy. | Written
by Mr. W. Shakespear. | [O. pendant bunch of fruit]
| London. | Printed in the Year 1710.

> Sm. 8vo. A–E, F⁵. pn. (1)–90. A stub to title A1.
> Printed for sale at The Hague and also forming a portion of vol. ii
> of *A Collection of the Best English Plays.*   (*S.*)

191. The | Merry Wives | of Windsor; | with the | Amours | of | Sir John Falstaff. | A | Comedy. | Written by Mr. W. Shakespear. | [O. monogrammic T.J.] | London, | Printed for the Company. [N.D. *c.* 1720.]

> Sm. 8vo. A–E, F⁴. pn. (1)–(88). p. 79 misnumbered 76. Printed for T. Johnson at The Hague, but type entirely reset from the 1710 edition. The text is similar.   (*B.M., B.H.*)

192. The | Merry Wives | of | Windsor. | A | Comedy. | = | By Mr. William Shakespear. | = | [O. SHO.] | = | London: | Printed for Jacob Tonson, in the Strand, | MDCCXXI.

> 12mo. A–C. pn. (1)–72. No F.   (*B.H., S.*)

193. The | Merry Wives | of | Windsor. | A | Comedy. | As it is Acted at the | Theatres. | = | By Mr. William Shakespear. | = | [O. ✳✳✳✳] | ≡ | Dublin: | Printed for A. Bradley, at the Golden-Ball and | Ring opposite Sycamore-Alley, in Dame-Street, Book-|seller, M.DCC.XXX.

> Sm. 8vo. A–D, E⁴. pn. (1)–72.
> The first Irish separate edition.   (*J. de L. S., Yale*)

194. The | Merry Wives | of | Windsor. | A | Comedy. | = | By Mr. William Shakespear. | = | [O. SHO.] | = | London: | Printed for J. Tonson: And Sold by W. Feales, | at Rowe's Head, the Corner of Essex-Street, in | the Strand. MDCCXXXIII.

> 12mo. A–C. pn. (1)–72, including F. by LDG.   (*P.&C., S.*)

195. The | Merry Wives | of | Windsor. | A | Comedy. | = | By Mr. William Shakespear. | = | [O. basket of fruit and flowers] | = | Southwark: | Printed and sold at the Printing Office, in | Angel-Court, near the King's Bench. 1734.

> 12mo, in sixes. A–F, G⁴. pn. (1)–80.
> A rare edition.   (*Adler*)

196. The | Merry Wives | of | Windsor. | A | Comedy. | = | By Mr. William Shakespear. | = | [O. SHO.] | = | London: | Printed for J. Tonson, and the rest of the Proprietors; | And Sold by the Booksellers of London and | Westminster, 1734.

> 12mo. A–C. pn. (1)–(72). Last leaf a blank. No F. and probably issued thus. Headline to p. 70 reads 'The Merry Wives &c.' Possibly the earliest issue of this play in the Tonson series, and before the piracy notice on last page. *Vide* 197, a similar imprint. There is no interpolation, l. 1, p. 34.   (*S.*)

197. The | Merry Wives | of | Windsor. | A | Comedy. | = | By Mr. William Shakespear. | = | [O. SHO.] | = | London, | Printed: And Sold by the Booksellers of London | and Westminster. 1734.

> 12mo. A–C. pn. (1)–(72). No F. issued with this. Headline to p. 70, 'The Merry Wives &c.' C12ᵛ has an advertisement, dated September 6, 1734, offering to sell plays at 'One Penny each Play', in competition with and to cut out R. Walker. 'Terrestrial' interpolation, l. 1, p. 34, omitted. The text entirely reset.   (*S.*)

198. The | Merry Wives | of | Windsor. | A | Comedy. | = | By Mr. William Shakespear. | = | [O. fruit spray] | ≡ | London: | [B] | MDCCXXXIV.

> 12mo. A–C. pn. (1)–(72), exclusive of LDG. F. (1728, 1714). CL. on recto of last leaf. The headline of p. 34 reads 'The Marry Wives' and l. 1 reads 'Terrestrial, so give me thy hand'. Type entirely reset.   (*B.H., S.*)

199. The | Merry Wives | of | Windsor. | A | Comedy. | = | By Mr. William Shakespear. | = | [O. basket of fruit and flowers] | ≡ | London: | [B] | MDCCXXXIV.

> 12mo. A–C. pn. (1)–(72), exclusive of LDG. F. (1728, 1714). Recto of last leaf TW. advertisement. The text is reset. pp. 34–5, the headline reads 'Of Windsor' 'The Merry Wives', and l. 1, p. 34, the interpolation reads 'Terestrial'.   (*S.*)

200. The | Merry Wives | of | Windsor. | A | Comedy. | As it is Acted at the | Theatres. | = | By Shakespear. |

= | [O. basket of fruit supported by female bust]
| = | London | [W. 1] MDCCXXXIV.

12mo. A, B, C⁶, D⁶, E². pn. (1)–76, exclusive of F. by J. Smith
after LDG. (*B.M.*)

201. The Merry Wives | of | Windsor. | A | Comedy. |
As it is Acted at the | Theatres. | = | By Shakespear
| = | [O. billing doves] | = | London: | [W. 3]
MDCCXXXIV.

12mo. A, B, C⁶, D⁶, E². pn. (1)–76, exclusive of F. by J. Smith.
Sc. V, Act III misprinted Sc. III. Type entirely reset with ornaments
differing from the 1734 [sic] edition of Walker's. Tp. cornucopiae
with birds. (*S.*)

202. The | Merry Wives | of | Windsor. | A | Comedy.
| As it is Acted at the | Theatres. | = | By Shakespear.
| = | [O. basket of fruit] | = | London: | [W. 1] 1734.

12mo. A⁶, a⁶, B¹², C⁶, D⁶, E². pn. (1)–76, exclusive of F. by Smith.
Scene V, Act III misprinted Scene III in some copies. C5 and D5
respectively printed C3 and D3. Tp., intaglio head in floriated
oval. p. 66 n. 56. (*B.H., S.*)

203. The | Merry Wives of Windsor, | A | Comedy.
| By Shakespeare. | = | Collated with the oldest Copies
and Corrected; | With Notes Explanatory, and Critical,
By Mr. Theobald. | = | I. Decus, i, nostrum [&c.]
Virg. | = | Dublin: | Printed for Abraham Bradley at |
the Two Bibles in Dames-street, Bookseller. | = |
M DCCXXXIX. |

12mo. ‡1, L–N, O⁷. pn. (215)–(302). Last page contains 'Books
Printed for A. Bradley'. In the list appear *King Henry VIII, Hamlet, Othello, Julius Caesar, Henry IV*, and *King Richard III*.
This is an issue of the play contained in vol. i of *The Works*,
by Theobald, Dublin, 1739, with a fresh title-page instead of the
half-title and with an advertisement printed on the last page—
which in the *Works* is a blank. (*B.M.*)

ADVERTISED BUT NOT RECORDED

The Merry Wives.

T. Astley . . . . 1728 or A.

A MIDSUMMER NIGHT'S DREAM

204. The | Comick Masque | of | Pyramus and Thisbe. | As it is Perform'd at the | Theatre in Lincoln's Inn Fields. | = | — Juvinum pulcherrimus [&c. 2 lines] | = | London: | Printed for W. Mears, at the Lamb without | Temple-Bar. MDCCXVI.

Narrow 4to. A–C. pn. 8 pp. n.n.+1–16. (*Adler*)

205. A | Midsummer-Night's | Dream. | = | By Mr. William Shakespear. | = | [O. winged Cupid's head over altar] | = | London: | [B] | MDCCXXXIV.

12mo. A–B, C^6. pn. (1)–60, exclusive of FO. F. (1728, 1714). (*B.M., B.H., S.*)

206. A | Midsummer-Night's | Dream. | A | Comedy. | = | By Shakespear. | = | [O. woman's head in decorated roundel] | = | London: | [W. 10] | MDCCXXXV.

12mo. A, B, C^6. pn. (1)–(60), exclusive of FO. F. re-engraved in reverse, probably by J. Smith. p. 59 misnumbered 11. (*B.M., P.&C., S.*)

207. A | Midsummer Night's | Dream, | A Comedy. | = | By Shakespeare. | = | [O. Neptune seated] | = | London: | Printed in the Year M.DCC.XXXV.

12mo. A, B, C^6. pn. (1)–(60), and in all particulars as Walker's 1735 edition, with misnumbered page 59, n. 11, except that the dramatis personae on the verso of the title are reset. (*S.*)

MUCH ADO ABOUT NOTHING

208. Much Ado | about | Nothing. | = | By Mr. William Shakespear. | = | [O. marigold spray] | = | London: | [A] | MDCCXXXIV.

12mo. A–C. pn. (1)–72, exclusive of LDG. F. (1728, 1714). (*B.M., B.H., S.*)

209. Much Ado | about | Nothing. | = | By Shakespear.

| = | [O. basket of flowers] | = | London: | [W. 11]
MDCCXXXV.

> 12mo. A–C. pn. (1)–72, exclusive of F. unsigned, depicting the
> same incident as 1714, 1728, but with a different setting.
> ado is printed so in six headlines. (*B.M., S.*)

210. Much Ado | about | Nothing. | = | By Shake-
speare. | = | [O. decorated vase of fruit] | = | London:
| Printed in the Year M.DCC.XXXV.

> 12mo. A–C. pn. (1)–72, exclusive of F., as in Walker's edition,
> 1735, and of which this is a reissue, except that the dramatis
> personae are reset. (*S.*)

211. The | Universal Passion. | A | Comedy. | As it
is Acted at the | Theatre-Royal | in | Drury-Lane,
| By His Majesty's Servants. | = | Amor Omnibus
Idem. Virg. Georg. Lib. 3. | ≡ | London: | Printed for
J. Watts at the Printing-Office in | Wild-Court, near
Lincoln's-Inn-Fields. MDCCXXXVII. | = | Price One
Shilling and Six Pence.

> 8vo. A⁴, B–E, F⁴, G⁴. pn. 8 pp. n.n.+(1)–(80). The last 4 pp.
> G3 and 4, contain an advertisement 'Books lately published'. These
> 2 leaves are lacking in the Bodleian copy. p. 75 numbered 76 and
> 76 n.n. Altered from *Much Ado about Nothing* by James Miller,
> and dedicated to F. Franckland. (*Bod., Folger*)

212. The | Universal Passion. | A | Comedy, | As it is
Acted at the | Theatre-Royal | in | Drury-Lane, | By His
Majesty's Servants. | = | — Amor Omnibus Idem.
Virg. Georg. Lib. 3. | ≡ | London Printed: And
Dublin Re-|printed by and for Sylvanus Pepyat, Book-
|seller, in Skinners-Row, M.DCC.XXXVII.

> 8vo, in fours. A–K, L². pn. (1)–84. The first 3 leaves, A–D, are
> signed, an uncommon procedure. 'Epilogue Spoken by Mrs Clive'
> on part of p. 82 and p. 83. On p. 84 an advertisement of Pepyat's
> productions. Dedication to F. Franckland not included in this
> edition.
> A very scarce edition. (*F. O'Kelley*)

OTHELLO

213. Othello, | The | Moor of Venice. | A | Tragedy. | As it hath been divers times Acted at the | Globe, and at the Black-Friers: | And now at the | Theatre Royal, | By Her Majesties Servants. | = | Written by W. Shakespear. | = | London: | Printed for R. Welling-ton, at the Dolphin and Crown, at the West-End | of St Paul's Church-Yard. 1705. | Newly publish'd Claudius Mauger's [&c. 9 lines].

> 4to. A², B–K, L². pn. 4 pp. n.n.+1–(76). On the recto of A2, 'Plays printed for and Sold by R. Wellington', include *Mackbeth, Timon of Athens, All for Love, Titus Andronicus, Antony and Cleopatra, Tempest, Caius Marius, Hamlet, Henry the Sixth, Julius Caesar, Othello, Richard the Second, Richard the Third, King Lear,* and on the last page, 'Shakespear's Plays in one Volume in Folio'.
> *(Adler)*

214. Othello, | The | Moor of Venice. | A | Tragedy. | Written by Mr. W. Shakespear. | [O. fountain with cattle drinking and motto 'Non sibi sed omnibus'] | London. | Printed in the Year 1710.

> Sm. 8vo. A–G, H². pn. (1)–(116). Last leaf a blank.
> Printed for T. Johnson at The Hague separately and also forming part of vol. i, *A Collection of the Best English Plays,* 1712. *(B.M., S.)*

215. Othello, | The | Moor of Venice. | A | Tragedy. | Written by Mr. W. Shakespear. | [O. monogrammic T. J.] | London, | Printed for the Company. [N.D. *c.* 1720.]

> Sm. 8vo. A–F, G⁶. pn. (1)–108.
> From the press that printed the 1710 edition for T. Johnson at The Hague. A similar text but entirely reset. *(B.H.)*

216. Othello, | The | Moor of Venice. | A | Tragedy. | = | By Mr. William Shakespear. | = | [O. globe and compasses floriated] | Dublin: | Printed by and for George Grierson, at the | Two Bibles in Essex-Street. 1721.

> Sm. 8vo. A–F. pn. (1)–96. In the alphabet D3 and D4 reversed. 'Essex-Street' in italics. *(T. Col. Dublin)*

217. Othello, | The | Moor of Venice; | A | Tragedy, | As it hath been divers times Acted at | the Globe, and at the Black-Friers: | And now at the Theater-Royal, by | His Majesty's Servants. | = | Written by W. Shakespear. | = | [O. conventional blocks] | = | London; | Printed by John Darby in Bartholomew-Close, for | Mary Poulson, and sold by A. Bettes-|worth in Pater-noster-Row, R. Caldwell in Newgate-street, and F. Clay without Temple-|Bar. M.DCC.XXIV. Price 1s.

12mo, in sixes. A–H. pn. (1)–96.   (*B.H., P.&C., S.*)

218. Othello, | The | Moor of Venice. | A | Tragedy. | = | By Mr. William Shakespear. | = | [O. dog baying at the moon] | = | Dublin: | Printed by and for George Grierson, at the | Two Bibles in Essex Street. MDCCXXV.

Sm. 8vo. A–F. pn. (1)–96.
Not a separate issue of Pope's edition published by Grierson, 1725–6, but a reprint of Rowe's text, 1714.   (*S.*)

219. Othello, | The | Moor of Venice. | A | Tragedy. | = | Written by Mr. Wil. Shakespear. | = | Revised and corrected by Mr. Pope. | = | [O. vase flanked by birds] | = | Dublin: | Printed by and for George Grierson, at the Two | Bibles in Essex-Street. M.DCC.XXVI.

The Title-page only, attached to *Hamlet* of the same date (No. 48). On the verso is the dramatis personae, no half-title. Catchword 'Othel.' If this follows the procedure adopted in publishing *Hamlet*, the collation should run 8vo. A⁴, B–G, H². pn. (1)–108.
     (*T. Col. Camb.*)

220. Othello, | The | Moor of Venice, | A | Tragedy. | = | By Mr. William Shakespear. | = | [O. SHO.] | = | London: | [A] | MDCCXXXIV.

12mo. A–D. pn. (1)–96, exclusive of LDG. F. (1728, 1714), basket of fruit on bracket Tp.   (*B.H., S.*)

221. Othello, | The Moor of Venice. | A | Tragedy. | = | By Mr. William Shakespear. | = | [O. basket of fruit with flower sprays] | ≡ | London: | [B] | MDCCXXXIV.

> 12mo. A–D. pn. (1)–96, exclusive of LDG. F. CS. replaces Tp. on the last p., and the type throughout the play entirely reset.
> p. 32 n. 23, 90 n. 91, 91 n. 90, 94 n. 95, 95 n. 94.
> (*B.M., B.H., S.*)

222. Othello, | The | Moor of Venice. | A | Tragedy. | As it is Acted at the | Theatres. | = | By Shakespear. | = | [O. intaglio woman's head ornamented] | = | London: | [W. 4] M.DCC.XXXIV.

> 12mo. A–D. pn. (1)–96, inclusive of F. by Smith (rare), and 2 leaves of advertisement at the end, offering 'Volume I unbound at 2/= or the Plays separately at 4ᵈ each'. With this volume is given a 'Head of Shakespear work'd in Colours', as well as a general title and an Account of the Life and writings of the Author.
> (*B.M., B.H., S.*)

223. Othello, | The | Moor of Venice. | A | Tragedy. | As it is Acted at the | Theatres. | = | By Shakespeare | = | [O. Britannia facing front] | = | London: | Printed in the Year M.DCC.XXXV.

> 12mo. A–C, D¹⁰. pn. (1)–92, inclusive of F. by Smith, and in all other respects as Walker's edition, except for advertisement leaves.
> (*B.H.*)

224. Othello, | The | Moor of Venice. | A | Tragedy, | As it is Acted at the | Theatres | = | By Shakespear. | = | [O. covered urn on floriated bracket] | = | London: | Printed in the Year M.DCC.XXXVI.

> 12mo. A–C, D¹⁰. pn. (1)–92, inclusive of F. A reissue of Walker's 1734 edition with a fresh title. (*B.H.*)

ADVERTISED BUT NOT RECORDED

Othello.

R. Wellington. 4to	.	.	.	. 1704 or A.
J. Astley. 12mo	.	.	.	. 1728 „
G. Risk, Ewing, and Smith	.	.	.	. 1729 „
W. Feales, Ewing, and Smith	.	.	.	. 1734 „
P. Crampton, Dublin (Popes)	.	.	.	. 1731 „

PERICLES

225. Pericles, | Prince | of | Tyre. | = | By Mr.
William Shakespear. | = | [O. vase of fruit, enfoliaged]
| = | London; | [A] | MDCCXXXIV.

> 12mo. A–C, D⁴. pn. (1)–(68), exclusive of FO. F. (1728, 1714).
> CL. on pp. 3 and 68, though set up differently. (*B.M.*, *B.H.*, *S.*)

226. Pericles, | Prince | of | Tyre. | = | By Shake-
spear. | = | [O. woman's head in decorated roundel]
| = | London: | [W. 5] MDCCXXXIV.

> 12mo. A, B, C⁶. pn. (1)–60, exclusive of FO. F. engraved in
> reverse by Smith. (*B.M.*, *B.H.*, *S.*)

227. Pericles | Prince | of | Tyre. | = | By Shakespeare.
| = | [O. tazza of flowers] | = | London: | Printed in the
Year M.DCC.XXXV.

> 12mo. A, B, C⁶. pn. (1)–60, exclusive of FO. F. engraved in
> reverse by Smith; except for title and dramatis personae exactly as
> Walker's 1734 edition. (*S.B.L.*, *S.*)

228. Marina: | A | Play | of | Three Acts. | As it is
Acted at the | Theatre Royal | in Convent-Garden. |
Taken from Pericles Prince of Tyre. | = | By Mr.
Lillo. | = | London: | Printed for John Gray, at
the Cross-Keys in the | Poultry, near Cheapside.
M.DCC.XXXVIII. | (Price One shilling.)

> 8vo, in fours. A–G, H². pn. (1)–60. (*P.&C.*)

THE PURITAN

229. The | Puritan: | or The | Widow | of | Watling-
Street. | = | By Mr. William Shakespear. | = | [O.
tazza of fruit with scrolls] | = | London; | [A] |
MDCCXXXIV.

> 12mo. A, B, C⁶. pn. (1)–60, exclusive of LDG. F. (1728, 1714).
> 'A3' printed 'B3'. Some copies p. 46 n.n. (*B.M.*, *B.H.*, *S.*)

230. The | Puritan: | or, The | Widow | of | Watling-Street. | A | Comedy. | = | By Shakespear. | = | [O. doves billing over a floriated ornament] | = | London: | [W. 9] | = | MDCCXXXIV.

12mo. A, B, C⁶. pn. (1)–(60), exclusive of a new plate as F. depicting five characters in mourning that open with Sc. 1, engraved by J. Smith. The last page is a blank. 'C2' and 'C3' are respectively printed 'C3' and 'C5'.

The B.M. copy has an advertisement leaf after C6. It is probably insititious. (*B.M., B.H., S.*)

ROMEO AND JULIET

231. The | History and Fall | of | Caius Marius. | A | Tragedy, | As it is Acted at the | Theatre Royal. | = | By Thomas Otway. | = | Qui color Albus erat nunc est contrarius Albo. | = | London, | Printed for Rich. Wellington, at the Dolphin and Crown in Paul's | Church-Yard, and E. Rumball in Covent-Garden. 1703. | = | Newly publish'd some Fables [&c. 6 lines].

4to. A–I. pn. 6 pp. n.n.+1–(66). (*Adler*)

231a. The | History and Fall | of | Caius Marius. | A | Tragedy. | = | Qui color Albus [&c.]. | = | [O. flowers] | = | Printed in the Year 1712.

12mo. From H¹⁰ to M². pn. (187)–(195)+196–(268). An excerpt from *The Works of Mr Thomas Otway*, 1712, 2 vols. (vol. ii). (*P.&C.*)

232. The | History and Fall | of | Caius Marius. | A | Tragedy. | = | Printed in the Year 1717.

12mo. H8 to H12, I to L11. pn. (183)–262.
An excerpt from 'The Works | of | Mr. Thomas Otway, | in Two Volumes. | [&c.] — London: | Printed for J. T. And Sold by W. Mears, J. | Brown and F. Clay, without Temple-Bar, 1718'. (*McLeish*)

233. The | History and Fall | of | Caius Marius. | A | Tragedy. | = | Qui color Albus erat nunc est con-

trarius Albo. | = | [O.] | = Printed in the Year
1722. |

12mo. From H8 to L11. pn. (183)–262.
An excerpt from 'The | Works of | Mr. Thomas Otway; | [vol. ii,
&c.] London: | Printed for D. Browne, J. Tonson, B. and S. |
Tooke, G. Strahan, and M. Poulson, 1722.   (*Boston*)

234. The | History and Fall | of | Caius Marius. | A
Tragedy. | = | By Tho. Otway. | = | Qui color [&c.]
| = | [O. conventional] | = | London: | Printed by
John Darby in Bartholomew-Close, for | Mary Poul-
son, and sold by A. Bettes-|worth in Pater-noster Row,
R. Caldwell | in Newgate-street, and F. Clay without
Temple-|Bar. M.DCC.XXIV. Price 1s.

12mo, in sixes. A–G. pn. (1)–(84). The last 2 leaves with a list of
'Books printed for M. Poulson', in which Shakespeare's plays
are advertised in 9 volumes.   (*P.&C.*)

235. The | History and Fall | of | Caius Marius. | A |
Tragedy. | = | By Thomas Otway. | = | Qui color,
[&c.] | = | [O.] | = | Dublin: | Printed by J. Watts,
and sold opposite the | Watch-House, the North-side
of College Green. | MDCCXXV.

12mo, in fours. A–K. pn. (1)–(80), of which the first 6 are n.n.;
the last p. contains an advertisement of books.
A scarce edition.   (*H.N.P.*)

236. The | History and Fall | of | Caius Marius. |
A | Tragedy. | = | Qui color Albus erat nunc est con-
trarius Albo | = | [O.] | = | Printed in the Year 1727. |

12mo. H8 to L11. pn. (8), (191)–262.
An excerpt from vol. ii of 'The | Works | of | Mr. Thomas
Otway; | . . . . London: | Printed for J. Tonson, G. Strahan,
B. Motte, | D. Browne; Richard, James, and Bethel Wel-|lington.
MDCCXXVIII. |'   (*P.&C.*)

237. The | History and Fall | of | Caius Marius. | A
| Tragedy. | = | Qui Color Albus [&c.] | = | [O.
arum floriated] | London: | Printed for W. Feales, at
Rowe's Head, the Corner of | Essex-street in the
Strand; R. Wellington, at the | Dolphin and Crown

near Temple-bar; J. Welling-|ton and A. Bettesworth
and F. Clay, in Trust for B. Wellington. MDCCXXXIII.

    12mo, in sixes. A², B², C–H. pp. (1)–80. F. by W. King after
Vanhaeken extra. This may also be found included in a collection
of Otway's *Works* of various dates published by Tonson, &c., 1736.
                                              (*B.H.*)

238. Romeo | and | Juliet. | = | By Mr. William
Shakespear. | = | [O. music trophy] | ≡ | London: |
[A] | MDCCXXXIV.

    12mo. A–C, D⁶. pn. (1)–84, exclusive of FO. F. (1728, 1714).
p. 71 n.n.   (*S.*)

239. Romeo | and | Juliet. | A | Tragedy. | = | By
Shakespear. | = | [O. woman's head in intaglio] | = |
London: | [W. 10] MDCCXXXV.

    12mo. A–C, D⁶. pn. (1)–(84), exclusive of F. after FO.
                                      (*B.H., B.M.*)

240. The | History and Fall | of | Caius Marius. | A |
Tragedy. | = | Qui color [&c.] | = | [O. vase of flowers]
| London: | Printed for W. Feales, at Rowe's Head the
Corner of | Essex-street in the Strand; A. Bettesworth
in | Pater-Noster-Row; F. Clay. at the Bible, R. Wel-
| lington, at the Dolphin and Crown, and C. Corbett, |
at Addison's Head, all without Temple-Bar; and | J.
Brindley, at the King's Arms in New Bond-street. | = |
MDCCXXXV.

    12mo. A–D. pn. (1)–(96), including F. by King after Vanhaecken.
                                      (*P.&C.*)

241. The History and Fall of Caius Marius.

    A copy for collation purposes not available.
    Excerpt from Otway's *Plays*, 12mo. J. and R. Tonson, 1736.

             ADVERTISED BUT NOT RECORDED

Romeo and Juliet.

	M. Wellington	.	.	.	. 1718 or A.
Caius Marius	T. Astley	.	.	.	. 1728 „
	G. Risk	.	.	.	. 1729 „

SIR JOHN OLDCASTLE

242. The | History | of | Sir John Oldcastle, | The good | Lord Cobham. | = | By Mr. William Shakespear. | = | [O. small v-shaped design] | ≡ | London: | [A] | MDCCXXXIV.

> 12mo. A–C. pn. (1)–72, exclusive of FO. F. (1728, 1714). TW. on verso of title. Misprint 'forc'd Invention' in the prologue. (*S.*)

243. The | History | of | Sir John Oldcastle, | The Good | Lord Cobham. | = | By Shakespear. | [O. woman's head in floriated roundel] | London: | [W. 8] MDCCXXXIV.

> 12mo. A–C. pn. (1)–72, exclusive of FO. F. re-engraved probably by J. Smith. Headline p. 67 'Olddastle'. (*B.M., B.H., S.*)

244. The | History | of | Sir John Oldcastle, | The Good | Lord Cobham. | = | By Shakespear. | = | [O. heart-shaped decoration with winged head above] | = | London: | Printed in the Year M.DCC.XXXV.

> 12mo. A–C. pn. (1)–72. Should probably have F. by Smith. A reissue of Walker's 1734 edition. (*B.M.*)

245. The | History | of | Sir John Oldcastle, | The Good | Lord Cobham. | = | By Shakespear. | = | [O. handled vase on a floriated bracket] | = | London: | Printed in the Year MDCCXXXVI.

> 12mo. A–C. pn. (1)–72, exclusive of FO. F. re-engraved, and except for title a reprint of Walker's 1734 edition in every particular. (*S.*)

TAMING OF THE SHREW

246. Sauny the Scot; or, The | Taming of the Shrew: | A | Comedy, | As it is now Acted at the Theatre | Royal in Drury Lane, By Her | Majesty's Company of Comedi-|ans. | = | Written by John Lacy Esq: | = | Then I'll cry out, swell'd with Poetick Rage, | 'Tis I John Lacy, have reform'd your Stage. | Prol. to the

Rehears. | = | London: | Printed for B. Bragge, in Pater-noster-row, 1708 | Price one Shilling six Pence.

> 4to. A–I. pn. 8 pp. n.n.+1–(64), last p. blank; including the half-title with imprint 'Sauny | the | Scot'. (*B.H.*)

247. Sauny the Scot: | Or, The | Taming of the Shrew. | A | Comedy. | As it is Acted | at the Theatre-Royal in Drury-Lane. | = | Written Originally by Mr. Shake-spear, | = | Alter'd and Improv'd by Mr. Lacey, | Servant to His Majesty. | = | London: | Printed for E. Curll at the Dial and Bible against | St. Dunstan's Church in Fleetstreet; A. Bettesworth at | the Red-Lyon on London-Bridge; and J. Richardson | at the King's-Head the Corner of Swithing's-Alley | in Corn-hill. 1714. Price 1s.

> 12mo. ‡1, B–D, E2. 2 pp. n.n.+(1)–(76), not including F. by P. la Vergne, engraved by M. Vdr Gucht. Last leaf, 'Books lately Published'. (*S.*)

248. The | Cobler | of | Preston. | As it is Acted at the | Theatre-Royal | in | Drury-Lane. | By His Majesty's Servants. | = | Written by Mr. Johnson. | = | London: | Printed by W. Wilkins, at the Dolphin in |Little-Britain; and Sold by W. Hinch-|cliffe, at Dryden's-Head under the Royal-|Exchange. 1716. | (Price One Shilling.)

> Narrow 4to. A–G. pn. 8 pp. n.n. +(1)–(48), including F. with motto 'Ne Sutor ultra Crepidam'. On the last p., list of 'Books Sold'. (*P.&C.*)

249. The | Cobler | of | Preston | [an exact reissue of the 1st London impression, 1716, except for the insertion after 'Johnson' on the title-page of 'The Second Edition' with an additional rule] 1716. | (Price One Shilling.)

> (*B.H.*)

250. The | Cobler | of | Preston. | As it is Acted at the Theatre-Royal | in | Drury-Lane. | By His Majesty's

Servants. | = | Written by Mr. Johnson. | = | Dublin: | Re-printed by Thomas Humes, over-against the | Bible on the lower End of Cork-Hill; And | Sold by the Booksellers, 1716.

> Sm. 8vo, in fours. A–D, E³. pn. (1)–(38), the numbered leaves being 6–36. Last leaf a blank. (*N.L.D.*)

251. The | Cobler | of | Preston. | A | Farce. | As it is Acted at the | New Theatre | in | Lincolns-Inn-Fields. | [Line of type ornaments] | By Mr. Christopher Bullock. | [Line of type ornaments] | London, | Printed for R. Palmer, at the Crown without | Temple-Bar, 1716. (Price 6d.) Where may be | had all sorts of Plays.

> 12mo, in sixes. A–C. pn. (i)–(xii)+(1)–(24), including the half-title. (*Folger*)

252. The | Cobler | of | Preston. | and the | Adventures | of | Half an Hour. | As they are Acted at the | Theatre-Royal | in | Lincoln's-Inn-Fields. | = | Written by Mr. Christopher Bullock. | = | The Fourth Edition. | = | London; | Printed for T. Corbett, at Addison's Head, | without Temple-Bar: And Sold by Mr. Graves, | at the Bible in St. James'-street; Mr. Meadows, | at the Angel in Cornhill; and Mr. Stagg in West-| minster-Hall. MDCCXXIII. | [Price One Shilling.]

> 12mo, in sixes. A–D, E⁴. pn. 12 pp. n.n.+(1)–(44). The Cobler finishes on p. 22. A2 is the half-title.
> Halliwell remarks in the B.H. copy '*very rare*'. (*B.H.*)

253. The | Cobler of | Preston, | As it is Acted at the | Theatres, with Applause | = | Written by Mr. John-son | = | [O.] | = | Dublin; | Printed by S. Powell, for George Risk at the Cor-|ner of Castle-lane in Dame's-street, near the Horse-guard. | MDCCXXV.

> 12mo. A⁶, B⁶, C⁴. pn. 28 pp.+4 n.n. (*N.L.D.*)

254. The | Cobler of Preston, | A | Farce. | As it is Acted at the | Theatre-Royal | in Lincoln's-Inn-Fields. | = | Written by Mr. Christopher Bullock. | = | The

Fifth Edition. | ≡ | London: | Printed for W. Feales, at Rowe's-Head in St. | Clement's Church-Yard. MDCCXXIX. | (Price Six Pence.)

> 12mo. A⁶–B⁶, C³. pn. (i)–vi+(7)–(30). C2 is a separate leaf, pasted in. On the last p., 'Plays sold by W. Feales', including *Hamlet* and *K. Lear*. (*Folger*)

255. Sauny the Scot: | or, The | Taming of the Shrew. | A | Comedy. | As it is Acted | at the Theatre-Royal | in Drury-Lane. | = | Written originally by Mr. Shake-spear. | = | Alter'd and Improv'd by Mr. Lacey, | Servant to His Majesty. | = | London: | Printed in the Year MDCCXXXI.

> 12mo. A–E, in sixes, F⁴. pn. (1)–(68), with F. unsigned. (*Folger*)

256. The | Cobler | of | Preston. | An | Opera, | As it is Acted at the | New Booth in Dublin, | With Great Applause. | = | — Sutor ultra Crepidam. Hor. | = | [O. common block] | = | Dublin: | Printed by George Faulkner in Essex-street, | opposite to the Bridge, MDCCXXXII.

> 8vo. A⁴, B⁴, C⁴, D⁶. pn. (1)–36, the last 3 n.n. p. 33 misnumbered 29. The 'Prologue spoken by Miss Woffington'. (*N.L.D., B.M.*)

257. The | Taming | of the | Shrew. | = | By Mr. William Shakespear. | = | [O. rabbit] | ≡ | London: | [A] | MDCCXXXIV.

> 12mo. A–C, D⁶. pn. (1)–84, exclusive of FO. F. (1728, 1714). T.W. on A2 recto. (*S.*)

258. The | Taming | of the | Shrew. | A | Comedy. | = | By Shakespear. | = | [O. woman's head intaglioed] | = | London: | [W. 10] MDCCXXXV.

> 12mo. A–C. pn. (1)–72, with re-engraved FO. F. extra.
> (*B.M., B.H.*)

259. The | Taming | of the | Shrew. | A | Comedy. | = | By Shakespeare. | = | [O. Britannia] | = | London: | Printed in the Year M.DCC.XXXV.

> 12mo. A–C. pn. (1)–72, exclusive of FO. F. re-engraved, probably

by J. Smith. Except for imprint of title and dramatis personae, a facsimile of Walker's edition of the same date, and probably printed by him. *(S.)*

260. Sauny the Scot: | or, The | Taming of the Shrew. | A | Comedy. | As it is Acted at the | Theatre-Royal | in | Drury-Lane. | = | Written Originally by Shake-spear. | = | Alter'd and Improv'd by Mr. Lacey, | Servant to His Majesty. | = | London: | Printed for W. Feales, at Rowe's-Head, over-|against St. Clement's Church in the Strand. | = | M.DCC.XXXVI.

12mo, in sixes. A–E, F⁴. pn. (1)–(68), with F. *(Folger)*

261. A | Cure | for a | Scold. | A | Ballad Farce | of | Two Acts. | (Founded upon Shakespear's taming | of a Shrew.) | As it is Acted by his Majesty's Com-|pany of Comedians at the Theatre Royal | in Drury Lane. | = | By J. Worsdale, Portrait-Painter. | ≡ | London: | Printed for L. Gilliver, at Homer's Head, | Fleetstreet. | (Price One Shilling.) [N.D. *c.* 1737.]

Narrow 4to. ‡1, A–G, H2. pn. 10 pp. n.n.+(1)–(60). There is a gap in numbering, pp. 17–24 being omitted. *(Adler)*

262. A | Cure | for a | Scold. | As it is now acting at the Theatres | in London and Dublin, with universal | Applause. | = | By Mr. Worsdale. | ≡ | [O. basket of flowers with sprays] | ≡ | Dublin: | Printed by George Faulkner, For the Author, and Sold by the Booksellers. | = | MDCCXXXVIII. | [Price a British Shilling.]

Narrow 4to. A², B–F, G². pn. 4 pp. n.n.+(1)–(44). The epilogue is on the last leaf with the verso blank.

No other copy of this date in B.M. *(Mich., B.M.)*

ADVERTISED BUT NOT RECORDED

Taming of the Shrew.

Sauny the Scot. W. Feales	. . . . .	1734 or A.
Cobler of Preston. G. Risk (Dublin)	. . .	1725 „
Cobler of Preston. G. Risk, G. Ewing, and W. Smith	1729 „

TEMPEST

263. The | Tempest: | or, The | Enchanted Island. | A | Comedy: | As it is now Acted, | By His | Majesties Servants. | ≡ | London, Printed for J. Tonson, and T. Bennet, and Sold by | R. Wellington, at the Dolphin and Crown at the West-|end of S. Paul's Church-yard, G. Strahan, over against | the Royal Exchange in Cornhil, and B. Lintott, at the | Post-house next the Middle-Temple Gate in Fleet-|street, MDCCI.

4to. A–H, I². pn. 6 pp. n.n.+1–(62).
Dryden and Davenant's version. (*Boston, Adler*)

264. ≡ | The | Tempest, | or, The | Enchanted Island. | ≡ | [half-title] [N.D. 1701]

Folio, in fours. Ff2ᵛ to Mm2ᵛ. pn. (226)–274.
An excerpt from vol. i,'The | Comedies, | Tragedies, | and | Operas | Written by | John Dryden, Esq; | ≡ | Now first Collected together, and | Corrected from the Originals. | ≡ | In Two Volumes. | ≡ | London, | Printed for Jacob Tonson, at Gray's-Inn-Gate in Gray's-Inn-Lane; | Thomas Bennet, at the Half-Moon; and Richard Wellington, at | the Lute in St. Paul's Church-Yard. MDCCI.
(*S.*)

265. The | Tempest: | or, The | Enchanted Island. | A | Comedy. | ≡ | First written by | Mr. William Shakespear. | & since altered by | Sr. William Davenant, | and | Mr. John Dryden. | [O. basket of flowers en-foliaged] | London, | Printed in the Year 1710.

Sm. 8vo. A–G. pn. (1)–112. p. 96 n. 94, 111 n. 101.
Printed, probably abroad, for T. Johnson at The Hague, and also published in vol. ii of *A Collection of the Best English Plays*, 1712.
(*S.*)

266. The | Tempest: | or, The | Enchanted Island. | A | Comedy. | As it is Acted at | His Highness the Duke of | York's Theater. | ≡ | [O. bear and clubs] | ≡ | Printed in the Year MDCCXVII. (*S.*)

12mo. G10 to L7. pn. (163)–(254).
An excerpt from vol. ii, 'The Dramatick | Works | of John Dryden Esq; | in | six volumes. | ≡ | London: | Printed for Jacob Tonson at

Shakespear's Head | over against Katharine-Street in the Strand. | MDCCXVII.'

Note that this edition of Dryden was again issued in 1718, the general title to vol. i was altered, the imprint being as follows: 'London: | Printed for J. Tonson: And Sold by J. Bro-|therton and W. Meadows, at the Black | Bull in Cornhill. MDCCXVIII.' The imprints to the other vols. and play-titles are the same as in the 1717 edition. (*S.*)

267. The | Tempest: | or, The | Enchanted Island. | A | Comedy. | = | First written by | Mr. William Shakespear. | & since altered by | Sr. William Dave-nant | and | Mr. John Dryden. | [O. T. J. intertwined] | London, | Printed for the Company. | [N.D. *c.* 1720]

Sm. 8vo. A–F, G⁴. pn. (1)–(106). The last 3 pp. contain 'Cata-logue of English Plays' and 'English Books'. Among the latter are Pope's *Poems and Miscellanies* (dated 1718) and 'Priors Poems compleat' (dated 1720). The list of English plays terminates at 'The Siege of Damascus'. pp. 81–2 are omitted in the paging; the actual pp. are 104. (*B.M., Mich.*)

268. The | Tempest. | A | Comedy | By Mr. William Shakespear. | = | Collated and Corrected by the | former Editions, | By Mr. Pope. | = | [O.] | = | Dublin: Printed by and for George Grierson, at the | Two Bibles in Essex-Street, and for George | Ewing at the Angel and Bible in Dames-Street. | MDCCXXV.; |

Sm. 8vo. A, B², C–F, G². pn. 20 pp. n.n.+(1)–(68).

Included in the collation and preceding the above is the second title to vol. i of Pope's 1726 edition by Grierson, and dated 1725 (q.v. p. 22). Leaf G2 is a blank with advertisement on the verso relating to the imminent publication of the whole works; this does not appear in the set.

A very scarce state. (*Rosenbach, Stockwell*)

269. The | Tempest: | or, The | Enchanted Island. | A | Comedy. | As it is Acted at | His Highness the Duke of | York's Theater. | = | [O. v-shaped scroll] | = | Printed in the Year MDCCXXV.

12mo. From G10 to L7. pn. (163)–(254), actual pn. commencing 172.

An excerpt from 'The Dramatick Works of John Dryden Esq. in six volumes. Vol. II. J. Tonson. 1725. London'. (*V.A.M.*)

270. The | Tempest: | or, The Enchanted Island. | A | Comedy. | As it is Acted at | His Highness the Duke of | York's Theatre. | = | [O. SHO.] | = | London: Printed for J. Tonson: and Sold by W. Feales at | Rowe's Head, the Corner of Essex-Street, in the Strand. | = | MDCCXXXIII.

12mo. A–D. pn. (1)–(96), including F. by LDG. the last leaf a blank. Dryden and Davenant's version. (*Adler, S.*)

271. The | Tempest. | = | By Mr. William Shakespear. | = | [O. SHO.] | ≡ | London: | [A] | MDCCXXXIV.

12mo. A, B, C⁶. pn. (1)–60, exclusive of F. by LDG. (1728, 1714). The type and printer's ornaments all differ from Tonson's other 1734 edition. (*B.H., S.*)

272. The | Tempest. | = | By Mr. William Shake-spear. | = | [O. lyre and crossed trumpets] | ≡ | London: [A] | MDCCXXXIV.

12mo. A, B, C⁶. pn. (1)–60, exclusive of LDG. F. Type completely reset. (*S.*)

273. The | Tempest. | A | Comedy. | = | By Shake-spear. | = | [O. basket of flowers] | = | London: | [W. 4] MDCCXXXIV.

12mo. A, B, C⁶. pn. (1)–60, exclusive of F. LDG. re-engraved by Smith in reverse. (*B.M., B.H., S.*)

274. The | Tempest: | or, The | Enchanted Island. | A | Comedy. | By Mr. Dryden. | = | [O. SHO.] | ≡ | London: | Printed for Jacob Tonson in the Strand. | = | MDCCXXXV.

12mo. I–M. pn. (169)–(264), including F. by G. Van der Gucht after Gravelot.
An excerpt from vol. ii, 'The Dramatick | Works | of | John Dryden, Esq. | —— | London: MDCCXXXV.' (*S.*)

275. The | Tempest: | [another edition 1735].

Title reset but reading as in the previous excerpt. Collation is the same, but the text, with ornaments, is entirely reset.
The 'hare' Hp. to the play, whereas to the other 'intaglio head in shell decoration'. 'Cupids trumpeting' Tp. to the one, and an interlaced scroll to the other. (*S.*)

276. The | Tempest: | 1735.

Issued as a separate play following closely that of Dryden's *Dramatick Works*, 1735 (q.v. 274), except that alphabet and pn. are altered to suit a separate entity. Title in red and black, but reading the same. 12mo. ‡2, A–C, D⁶. 86 pp. F. extra. (*P.&C.*)

277. The | Tempest. | = | By Mr. William Shakespear. | = | [O. winged Cupid's head over altar] | ≡ | London: | [B] | MDCCXXXVI.

12mo. A, B, C⁶. pn. (1)–60, exclusive of LDG. F. The text is entirely reset. (*B.M., S.*)

ADVERTISED BUT NOT RECORDED

The Tempest.

J. Darby for M. Wellington . . . . 1718 or A.

THOMAS, LORD CROMWELL

278. The | Life and Death | of | Thomas, | Lord Cromwell. | = | By Mr. William Shakespear. | = | [O. SHO.] | ≡ | London: | [A] | MDCCXXXIV.

12mo. A–C. pn. 24 pp. n.n. +(1)–(48), exclusive of LDG. F. (1728, 1714). The last 3 pp. blank. 'Some | Account of the Life, etc | of | Mr. William Shakespear. | Written by Mr. Rowe. | [being the abbreviation by Pope]' occupies A2 to A12. On the verso is the dramatis personae to the play. A F. portrait by LDG. (1728, 1714) often accompanies the 'Life'. (*B.H., S.*)

279. The | Life and Death | of | Thomas, | Lord Cromwell. | = | By Mr. William Shakespear. | = | [O. basket of fruit and flowers] | ≡ | London: | [B] | MDCCXXXIV.

12mo. A–C. pn. 24 pp. n.n.+(1)–(50), exclusive of LDG. F.

(1728, 1714). On the last p. TW. advertisement. The 'Life' occupies A2 to A9, followed by a blank page with dramatis personae printed on the verso. The text to the 'Life' and the play are both entirely reset. Some copies were published without the 'Life': in that case collation reads 12mo, ‡³, B–C. pn. 4 pp. n.n. +(1)–(50). A portrait by LDG. (1714, 1728) should accompany the 'Life'. The type and setting varies from the other Tonson edition of the same year. (*B.M., S.*)

280. The | Life | and | Death | of | Thomas Lord Cromwell. | A | Tragedy. | = | By Shakespear. | = | [O. two-handled vase on a decorated bracket] | = | London: | [W. 4] MDCCXXXIV.

12mo. A–B. pn. (1)–48, exclusive of LDG. F. re-engraved in reverse by Smith. A1 is a blank leaf and generally missing. (*B.M., B.H., S.*)

TIMON OF ATHENS

281. The | History | of Timon of Athens, | The Man-Hater. | As it is Acted | By Her Majesties Servants. | Made into a | Play. | = | By Tho. Shadwell. | = | London, | Printed by Tho. Warren, for Henry Herringman, and Sold | by Thomas Bennet, at the Half-Moon in St. Paul's | Church-Yard, 1703.

4to. A–I, K². pn. 6 pp. n.n.+1–(70). (*Adler*)

282. The | History | of | Timon of Athens, | The Man-Hater. | As it is Acted | By | Her Majesty's Servants. | Made into a | Play. | = | By Tho. Shadwell. | = | London: Printed and Sold by H. Hills, in Black-|Fryars, near the Water-side. [N.D. *c.* 1709.]

12mo. A–C, D⁸. pn. 1–(88).
This edition has been generally registered as *c.* 1700. It is certainly not so early; probably 1709, when H. Hills was using this imprint and at his zenith as a piratical publisher. (*B.H., S.*)

282a. 282 was entirely reprinted. The format and text are practically identical except for misspellings. A definite clue is that on p. 5 the penultimate line reads 'He'll' instead of 'Hee'll', and 'A3' is under 'suddenly' instead of 'what'. Collated from a copy lacking the title. (*S.*)

283. The History | of | Timon of Athens, | The
Man-Hater. | First writen by Mr. Wil. Shakespear, |
& since altered by Mr. Tho. Shadwell. | [O. mono-
grammic T. J. device] | Printed for T. Johnson, |
Bookseller at the Hague. | = | M.DCC.XII.

> Sm. 8vo. A–F, G⁶. pn. (1)–(108). (*B.H., S.*)

284. The | History | of | Timon of Athens, | The
Man-Hater. | First written by Shakespear, | and since
altered by T. Shadwell. | London: | Printed for the
Company. (N.D. *c.* 1720.)

> 12mo. 92 pp.
> An extract from Jaggard's Bibliography, but not located, possibly
> a Hague reprint published by Scheurleer *c.* 1750.   (*B.H.*)

285. The | History | of | Timon of Athens, | The Man-
Hater. | As it is Acted at the | Duke's Theatre. | Made
into a Play. | ≡ | Printed in the Year MDCCXX.

> 12mo. N–Q. pn. (289)–(384).
> An excerpt from vol. ii, 'The | Works | of | Thomas Shadwell,
> Esq; | ——— | = | London: | Printed for James Knapton, at the
> Crown in | St Paul's Church-Yard; and Jacob Tonson, | at Shake-
> spear's Head over-against Katharine-Street | in the Strand. MDCCXX.'
>   (*B.H.*)

286. Timon of Athens; | or The | Man-Hater, | As it
is acted at the | Theatre-Royal | in | Drury-Lane, |
By His Majesty's Servants. | = | By Thomas Shadwell.
| = | [O.] | London: | Printed for and Sold by the
Booksellers in Town | and Country, 1732. |

> 12mo, in sixes. A², B–H, I⁴. pn. 4 pp. n.n.+1–(92), not
> including F.   (*Boston*)

287. The | History | of | Timon of Athens, | The |
Man-Hater. | As it is Acted at the | Duke's Theatre. |
Made into a Play. | ≡ | London: | Printed in the Year
MDCCXXXII.

> 12mo, in sixes. A⁴, B–G, H⁴. pn. 8 pp. n.n., +(1)–(80). No
> F. with this.
> This is an entirely different edition from that of the Booksellers,
> 1732. Both of them are scarce.   (*B.H.*)

288. Timon of Athens, | A | Tragedy. | = | By Mr. William Shakespear. | = | [O. SHO.] | | ≡ | London: | [A] | MDCCXXXIV.

    12mo. A–C. pn. (1)–72, exclusive of FO. F. (1728, 1714). CS. below the dramatis personae on verso of title.   (*B.M., B.H., S.*)

289. Timon | of | Athens. | A | Tragedy. | = | By Shakespear, | = | [O. sun framed in cornucopiae] | = | London: | [W. 10] MDCCXXXV.

    12mo. A–C. pn. (3)–(72), with FO. F. re-engraved extra. p. 68 is a blank, followed by 4 pp. of Walker's advertisement ending 'All the Plays publish'd by him [J. Tonson] and his Accomplices are pirated incoherent Nonsense, and Grub-street Stuff'. Some copies bound up in the sets lack these 4 pp. Though commencing p. (3), there are actually 72 pp. as pp. 25, 26 are duplicated, the alphabet A being misprinted A3–A6 instead of A2–A5. B1 is printed C.   (*B.M., B.H., S.*)

290. Timon of Athens. | A | Tragedy. | = | By Shakespeare, | = | [O. rising sun] | = | London: | Printed in the Year MDCCXXXV.

    12mo. A, B, C¹⁰. pn. (1)–(68), including FO. F. re-engraved. Printed by R. Walker.   (*H.N.P.*)

291. The | History | of Timon of Athens, | The | Man-Hater. | = | Altered by Mr. Shadwell. | = | [space] | = | London: Printed for W. Feales, at Rowe's Head, over-|against St. Clement's Church in the Strand. | = | MDCCXXXVI.

    12mo, in sixes. A⁴, B–G, H⁴. pn. 8 pp. n.n., +(1)–(80), exclusive of F. by FO.   (*P. & C.*)

292. Timon | of | Athens: | or | The Man-Hater. | = | Written by Mr. W. Shakespeare. | = | Collated with the Oldest Copies, and Corrected; with | Notes Explanatory and Critical, | By Mr. Theobald. | ≡ | Dublin: | Printed by R. Reilly, | for Abraham Bradley, at the Two | Bibles in Dame's-Street. | = | M.DCC.XXXIX.

    12mo. A–C, D⁴. pn. (1)–80.
A reissue of the play published in vol. v of the *Works*, Theobald,

Dublin, 1739, with a fresh title in place of the half-title, but alphabet and pagination different. Possibly the type was reset. Has the catchword 'Titus' on p. 80. *(Folger)*

293. The | History of | Timon of Athens, | The | Man-Hater. | = | Altered by Mr. Shadwell. | = | [O. basket of fruit and flowers] | = | London: | Printed for the Booksellers in Town and Country. | = | MDCCXL.

12mo, in sixes. ‡⁴, X–Dd, ‡1. pn. 8 pp. n.n. 241–(326)+F. Last leaf a blank. 'Cc2' printed 'C2'. Dramatis personae, with Betterton as Timon.
An excerpt from Shadwell's *Plays*, 1740? *(B.H.)*

ADVERTISED BUT NOT RECORDED

Timon of Athens.

R. Wellington. 4to.	. . . . .	1704 or A.
J. Darby for M. Wellington	. . .	1718 ,,
W. Feales .	. . . . .	1734 ,,

TITUS ANDRONICUS

294 = | Titus | Andronicus. | = | [Colophon] London: | [B] | MDCCXXXIV.

12mo. A–C. pn. (1)–(72), exclusive of LDG. F. CL. on p. (70) and last leaf a blank. Published with half-title only. *(B.M., S.)*

295. = | Titus | Andronicus. | = | [Colophon] London: | Printed for J. Tonson, and the rest of the Proprie-|tors; And Sold by the Booksellers of London | and Westminster, 1734.

12mo. A–C. pn. (1)–(72), exclusive of LDG. F. (1728, 1714). CL. on p. (70) and last leaf a blank. The colophon is a slip pasted on, and this appears to be the only difference. The title is without imprint as 294. *(B.H., S.)*

296. Titus | Andronicus. | A | Tragedy. | As it is Acted at the | Theatres. | = | By Shakespear. | = | [O.

woman's head in floriated roundel] | = | London: |
[W. 4] MDCCXXXIV.

> 12mo. A–B, C¹⁰. pn. (1)–68, exclusive of LDG. F. re-engraved
> by Smith. On p. 68 is a note by Walker regarding the near publica-
> tion of Ravenscroft's adaptation, which was probably never printed.
> In some copies 54 n. 57 printed on inner margin, also 58 so.
>
> (*B.M., B.H., S.*)

297. Titus Andronicus. | A | Tragedy. | As it was
Acted at the | Theatre-Royal. | = | By Shakespeare.
| = | [O. mask framed and decorated] | = | London: |
Printed in the Year M.DCC.XXXV.

> 12mo. A, B, C¹⁰. pn. (1)–68, exclusive of LDG. F. re-engraved by
> Smith, and containing Walker's advertisement in regard to Ravens-
> croft's adaptation. A reissue of his 1734 edition with a fresh title
> and dramatis personae. (*S.*)

298. Titus Andronicus | A | Tragedy, | As it is Acted
at the | Theatres. | = | By Shakespear. | [O.] | = |
London | Printed in the Year MDCCXXXVI.

> 12mo. A, B, C¹⁰. pn. (1)–68, exclusive of LDG. F. re-engraved
> by Smith. Printed by R. Walker and as 297. (*H.N.P.*)

ADVERTISED BUT NOT RECORDED

Titus Andronicus.

R. Wellington. 4to.　　.　　.　　.　　.　　.　　1705 or A.

TROILUS AND CRESSIDA

299. Troilus and Cressida: | or, | Truth found too
late. | = | [1701]

> Folio, in fours. Cc4 to Kk4. pn. 199–256. An excerpt from vol. ii
> Dryden's *Works*, 1701 (vide *All for Love*).

300. The | Siege | of Troy, | A Tragi-Comedy, | As
it has been often Acted with | great Applause [&c.]
| = | [O. lyre and trumpets] | ≡ | London, | Printed in
the Year MDCIII. [sic] [1703].

> Sm. 12mo. A. pn. (1)–24.
> The last portion of 'The New History | of the | Trojan Wars [&c.]
> London, Printed for C. Bates, at the Sun and | Bible in Pye Corner.
> Price Bound 1s.' (*Bod.*)

300a. Issued again with imprint 'Printed in the Year MDCCXVIII'.
Attributed to E. Settle. *(Bod.)*

301. The | Siege | of | Troy, | A Tragy-Comedy, |
As it has been often Acted with | great Applause. |
Containing | A Description of all the Scenes, Machines,
| and Movements, with the whole Deco|ration of the
Play, | and Particulars of | the Entertainment. | London:
| Printed in the Year MDCCVIII.

    Sm. 4to. A–C. pn. (1)–24. *(Rosenbach)*

302. The | Siege | of Troy, | A Dramatick Perfor-
mance, | Presented in Mrs Mynn's Great Booth, in |
the Queen's-Arms-Yard near the | Marshalsea-Gate in
Southwark, du-|ring the Time of the Fair. | Contain-
ing | A Description of all the Scenes, Machines, | and
Movements, with the whole Deco-|ration of the Play
and Particulars | of the Entertainment. | = | [O. rooks
inverted] | = | London: | Printed by S. Lee, at the
White Swan in West-Smithfield, | and Sold by J.
Morphew near Stationers-Hall. [1715.]

    Narrow 4to. A², B, C, D². pn. (1)–(24). (lacking date, *B.M.*)

303. Troilus | and | Cressida: | or, | Truth found too
late. | A | Tragedy. | As it is Acted at the | Duke's
Theatre. | = | To which is Prefix'd, A Preface con- |
taining the Grounds of Criticism in Tragedy. | = |
Rectius, Iliacum [&c. 2 lines]. Hor. | = | Printed in
the Year MDCCXVII.

    12mo. A3 to F1. pn. (5)–(122), of which 5–14 are n.n., 119 n. 11.
An excerpt from vol. v of 'The Dramatick | Works | of John
Dryden Esq; | —— London: | Printed for Jacob Tonson at
Shakespear's Head | over against Katharine-Street in the Strand. |
MDCCXVII.' *(S.)*

304. Troilus | and | Cressida:—Printed in the Year
MDCCXXV.

    This is an excerpt from vol. v of Dryden's *Dramatick Works* of that
date. The title reads as the 1717 edition (q.v. No. 303), and the

text is a reissue similar in all respects. Dramatis personae, with
Betterton as Troilus, and Mrs. Mary Lee as Cressida.   (*B.H.*)

305. The | Siege | of | Troy, | A Tragi-Comedy, | As
it has been often Acted with | Great Applause. | Con-
taining | A Description of all the Scenes, Machines; |
and Movements, with the whole Deco-|ration of the
Play, and Particulars of | the Entertainment. | = | [O.
two horns across a lyre] | ≡ | London: | Printed in the
Year, MDCCXXVIII.

> Sm. 12mo. A. pn. (1)–24.
> Published with | The New | History | of the | Trojan Wars | and
> Troy's Destruction. | = | In Four Books. | = | ——— | = | To which
> is Added, | The Siege of Troy ——— Applause. | = | London, Printed
> for C. Bates, at the Sun and | Bible in Pye-Corner. Price Bound 1s. |
> 'The History' collates 12mo. A–F, pn., including woodcut F.
> (1)–144. There are 3 other woodcuts in the text.
> The *Siege of Troy* is attributed to Elkanah Settle. This edition does
> not appear to have been previously recorded.   (*S.*)

306. Troilus | and | Cressida. | A | Tragedy. | = | By
Mr. William Shakespear. | = | [O. rabbit] | ≡ |
London: | [A] | MDCCXXXIV.

> 12mo. A–D. pn. (1)–96, exclusive of FO. F. (1728, 1714).
>   (*B.M., B.H., S.*)

307. Troilus | and | Cressida. | A | Tragedy. | = | By
Shakespear. | = | [O. intaglio woman's head] | = |
London: | [W. 10] MDCCXXXV.

> 12mo. A–D. pn. (1)–96, exclusive of re-engraved FO. F.
>   (*B.M., B.H.*)

308. Troilus and Cressida: | or, | Truth found too
late, | A | Tragedy. | By Mr. Dryden. | = | To which is
Prefix'd A Preface Contain-|ing the Grounds of Critic-
ism in Tragedy. | = | Rectius. Iliacum [&c.] Hor.
| = | [O. SHO.] | ≡ | London: | Printed for J. Tonson
in the Strand. | = | MDCCXXXV.

> 12mo. A2 to E. 39 pp. n.n., including F.+42–120. An excerpt
> from vol. v of Dryden's *Dramatick Works*, 1735, Tonson. This is
> sometimes found bound up as a separate play but really is not so.
>   (*B.H.*)

TWELFTH NIGHT

309. Love Betray'd; | Or, The | Agreable Disappoint-
ment. | A | Comedy. | As it was Acted at the | Theatre
in Lincoln's-Inn-Fields. | = | By the Author of The
Ladies Visiting-Day. | = | Jam te sequetur. | = |
London: | Printed for D. Brown at the Black-Swan
without Temple-Bar, | F. Coggan in the Inner-Temple-
Lane, Fleet-Street, W. Davis at the | Black-Bull, and
G. Strahan at the Golden-Ball against the Ex-|change
in Cornhill. 1703.

> 4to. †, a, B–I. pn. 16 pp. n.n.+ 1–(64), with the half-title reading
> as first 3 lines of title. Advertisement of 'Books Printed' on a₄ and
> I4. By C. Burnaby. *(P.&C.)*

310. Twelfth-Night: | or, | What you Will. | = | By Mr.
William Shakespear. | = | [O. basket of fruit | ≡ |
London: | [B]‖ MDCCXXXIV.

> 12mo. A–C. pn. (1)–(72), exclusive of FO. F. (1728, 1714). On
> the recto of the last leaf, T.W. p. 63 n.n. *(B.M., B.H., S.)*

311. Twelfth-Night: | or, | What you Will. | = | By
Shakespear. | = | [O. basket of flowers] | = | London:
| [W. 11] MDCCXXXV.

> 12mo. A–C. pn. (1)–72, exclusive of FO. F. re-engraved in re-
> verse. p. 56 n. 54. Last leaf a blank. *(B.M., B.H., S.)*

TWO GENTLEMEN OF VERONA

312. The Two | Gentlemen | of | Verona. | = | By
Mr. William Shakespear. | = | [O. rabbit with scroll]
| ≡ | [A] | MDCCXXXIV.

> 12mo. A–C. pn. (1)–(72), exclusive of FO. F. (1728, 1714). CS.
> on A2 recto. *(B.H., S.)*

313. The Two | Gentlemen | of | Verona. | A | Comedy.
| = By Shakespear. | = | [O. woman's head in roundel
floriated] | = | London: | [W. 5] MDCCXXXIV.

> 12mo. A–B, C⁶. pn. (1)–60, including FO. F. re-engraved by
> Smith. 17 of the headlines printed 'two'. *(B.M., S.)*

314. The Two | Gentlemen | of | Verona. | A Comedy. | = | By Shakespeare. | = | [O. winged Cupid above heart-shaped ornament] | = | London: | Printed in the Year MDCCXXXV.

12mo. A–B, C⁶. pn. (1)–60, including FO. F. re-engraved by Smith.
This edition was printed by Walker, and differs from that of 1734 only in the title and dramatis personae, which are reset. (*S*.)

WINTER'S TALE

315. The | Winter's | Tale. | = | By Mr. William Shakespear. | = | [O. acorn ornament] | ≡ | London: | [B] | MDCCXXXV.

12mo. A–C, D⁶. pn. (1)–84, exclusive of FO. F. (1728, 1714).
(*B.M., B.H., S.*)

316. The | Winter's | Tale. | = | By Shakespear. | = | [O. basket of flowers] | = | London: | [W. 11] MDCCXXXV.

12mo. A–C, D⁶. pn. (1)–84, exclusive of FO. F. re-engraved in reverse probably by Smith. (*B.M., B.H., S.*)

YORKSHIRE TRAGEDY

317. A | Yorkshire | Tragedy. | = | By Mr. William Shakespear. | = | [O. a v-shaped scroll] | ≡ | London: | [A] | MDCCXXXV.

12mo. A. pn. (1)–(24), exclusive of F. unsigned (1728, 1714).
Last leaf a blank. (*B.M., B.H., S.*)

318. A | Yorkshire | Tragedy. | = | By Shakespear. | = | [O. woman's head in roundel floriated] | = | [W. 12] M.DCC.XXXV.

12mo. A. pn. (1)–(24), exclusive of F. re-engraved in reverse.
Last leaf a blank and p. 9 n.n. (*B.M., B.H., S.*)

DOUBLE FALSHOOD

319. Double Falshood; | or, | The Distrest Lovers. | A | Play, | As it is Acted at the | Theatre-Royal | in | Drury-Lane. | = | Written Originally by W. Shake-speare; | And now Revised and Adapted to the Stage | By Mr. Theobald, the Author of Shakespeare Restor'd. | = | Quod optanti [&c. 2 lines] Virg. | = | London: | Printed by J. Watts, at the Printing Office in | Wild-Court near Lincoln's-Inn Fields. | = | MDCCXXVIII.

> 8vo. A–E. 16 pp. n.n.+(1)–64.
> A1 contains the half-title. | = | Double Falshood; | or, | The Distrest Lovers. | = | A | [Price 1s. and 6d.] with the licence, 1727, on verso. (*S.*)

319a. The variation in the second edition is that immediately above the imprint is a rule and 'The Second Edition', in all other respects being a reissue. (*Folger*)

320. Double Falshood: or, The Distrest Lovers. | A | Play, | As it is Acted at the | Theatre-Royal | in | Drury-Lane. | = | Written Originally by W. Shake-speare; | And now Revised and Adapted to the Stage | By Mr. Theobald, The Author of Shake-|speare Restor'd. | = | Quod optanti [&c. 2 lines.] | = | Dublin: | Printed by and for J. Hyde and E. Dobson, and | for T. Benson, at Shakespeare's Head in Castle-|Street. MDCCXXVIII.

> 12mo. A–C. pn. 14 pp. n.n.+(1)–58. (*B.M.*)

ACKNOWLEDGEMENTS

BUT for the foundation laid by W. Jaggard in his *Shakespeare Bibliography* this collation would have entailed much more labour, and in the hope that it may supplement his monumental work I will bring this most pleasurable task to a conclusion by an expression of gratitude for the assistance accorded me. After such princely courtesy there is little largess at my bestowal except hearty thanks to those who have given me of their time, as well as records of their treasures. To mention only a few:

I am particularly beholden to Dr. R. B. McKerrow, Secretary of the Bibliographical Society, H. Sellers, Esq., of the British Museum, H. M. Cashmore, Esq., City Librarian, Birmingham, Percy Simpson, Esq., of Oriel College, Oxford, E. N. Adler, Esq., London, J. de Lacey Smyth, Dublin, M. M. Nyhoff of The Hague, The National Library, Dublin, and others at Oxford and Cambridge; D. Massey of Messrs. Pickering & Chatto, Ltd., Messrs. Dobells, Maggs Bros., and Bernard Quaritch, Ltd. In the United States the Boston, Folger, and Michigan Libraries, and lastly but not least, H. N. Paul, Esq., of Philadelphia, and G. E. Dawson, Esq., of Washington, have willingly given me particulars of some of the scarcer items not easily available on this side the Atlantic. In proofing my crude English the assistance of Mr. Simpson has been invaluable, and Dr. Johnson of the University Press has spared no pains to make this a comely and to be hoped a useful volume.

The Farewell

'Now the faire Goddesse Fortune, Fall deepe
in love with thee. . . . Prosperity be thy
Page.'—*Cor.* Act I, Sc. v.

AN INDEX OF THE SEPARATE PLAYS

INCLUDING THE ADAPTATIONS, AND EXCERPTS OF THE
LATTER.

(Excerpts are printed in italics.)

[Each series of plays is printed in chronological order, therefore varying in places from this index.]

All's Well, 1734, [2]1735.

Antony and Cleopatra, [2]1734.
    Beauty the Conqueror (Sedley's), *1702*.
    Antony and Cleopatra (Sedley's), *1722*.
    All for Love (Dryden's), *1701, 1703, 1709, 1710,* [2]*1717,* [2]*1720, 1725, 1727, 1728, 1730, 1731,* [2]*1735, 1740.*
    Caesar in Egypt (Cibber's), 1725, 1736.

As You Like It, 1734, 1735.
    Love in a Forest (Johnson's), *1723*.
    The Modern Receipt (Carrington and Bellamy), 1739.

The Comedy of Errors, 1734, 1735.

Coriolanus, 1734, [2]1735.
    The Invader of his Country (Dennis's), 1720, 1721. .

Cymbeline, 1734, 1735.

Hamlet, [3]1703, 1710, 1712, 1718, 1720, 1721, 1723, 1726, 1731, 1733, [7]1734, [2]1736, 1737, 1739.

Julius Caesar (including Dryden's and Davenant's), 1711, [3]1719, c. 1720, 1721, [2]1726, 1729, [4]1734, 1739.
    Julius Caesar (Sheffield's), *1722, 1722, 1726, 1729, 1740.*
    Marcus Brutus (Sheffield's), *1722, 1726, 1729, 1740.*

Henry IV, Pt. I, 1700, 1710, 1721, 1723, 1731, 1732, [2]1734, 1736, 1739.

Henry IV, Pt. II, c. 1720, 1733, [2]1734, 1735, 1736.

Henry V, 1734, [2]1735, 1736.
    Henry V (Hill's), 1723, 1724. (Orrery's) *1739*.
    Half Pay Officer, 1720.

Henry VI, Pt. I, [2]1735.

Henry VI, Pt. II, 1734, 1735, 1736.
    Humfrey, Duke of Gloucester (Philips's), [3]1723.

Henry VI, Pt. III, 1734, 1735, 1736.
    An Historical Tragedy (T. Cibber's), c. 1722, 1724.

Henry VIII, 1732, [3]1734, 1735, 1736, 1739.

King John, [2]1734, 1735, 1736.

Titus Andronicus, [3]1734, 1735, 1736.
Troilus and Cressida, 1734, 1735.
    Troilus and Cressida (Dryden's), *1701, 1717, 1725, 1735.*
    Siege of Troy (Settle's), 1703, 1708, 1715, 1718, 1728.
Twelfth Night, 1734, 1735.
    Love Betray'd (Burnaby's), 1703.
Two Gentlemen of Verona, [2]1734, 1735.
Winter's Tale, [2]1735.
Yorkshire Tragedy, [2]1735.
Double Falshood (Theobald's), [3]1728.

The figures preceding the dates indicate the number of editions or issues, and most of the location notes to the plays are not to be regarded as evidence of scarcity. In addition to the copies examined at the libraries or in other collections, about one-half of the separate plays, and all the sets except Pope's first London and Dublin editions, have been collated from those in the writer's collection, of which many are in duplicate.